Current Topics in Technology: Social, Legal, Ethical, and Industry Issues for Computers and the Internet

THIRD EDITION

Maureen Sheehan Paparella

Eugene Simko

COURSE TECHNOLOGY
CENGAGE Learning™

Australia • Brazil • Japan • Korea • Mexico • Singapore • Spain • United Kingdom • United States

COURSE TECHNOLOGY
CENGAGE Learning™

Current Topics in Technology: Social, Legal, Ethical, and Industry Issues for Computers and the Internet, Third Edition
Maureen Sheehan Paparella
Eugene Simko

Executive Editor: Kathleen McMahon

Senior Product Manager: Mali Jones

Associate Product Manager: Jon Farnham

Editorial Assistant: Lauren Brody

Director of Marketing: Cheryl Costantini

Marketing Manager: Tristen Kendall

Marketing Coordinator: Julie Schuster

Print Buyer: Julio Esperas

Content Project Manager: Matthew Hutchinson

Proofreader: Suzanne Huizenga

Compositor: GEX Publishing Services

Printer: Globus

For product information and technology assistance, contact us at
Cengage Learning Customer & Sales Support, 1-800-354-9706

For permission to use material from this text or product, submit all requests online at **www.cengage.com/permissions**
Further permissions questions can be emailed to
permissionrequest@cengage.com

ISBN-13: 978-1-4390-3870-3

ISBN-10: 1-4390-3870-8

Course Technology
20 Channel Center Street
Boston, MA 02210
USA

Cengage Learning is a leading provider of customized learning solutions with office locations around the globe, including Singapore, the United Kingdom, Australia, Mexico, Brazil, and Japan. Locate your local office at:
international.cengage.com/region

Cengage Learning products are represented in Canada by Nelson Education, Ltd.

To learn more about Course Technology, visit **www.cengage.com/coursetechnology**

To learn more about Cengage Learning, visit **www.cengage.com**

Purchase any of our products at your local college store or at our preferred online store **www.ichapters.com**

Printed in the United States of America
1 2 3 4 5 6 7 15 14 13 12 11 10 09

CURRENT TOPICS IN TECHNOLOGY
Contents

PREFACE

Learning Goals and Objectives

Traditional information technology courses stress the mechanics of "how things work" within a fundamental conceptual framework, both on the computer and across the ether of the Internet. The supplemental use of current technology topics, as covered in various media, will "bring alive" subject matter addressed within the curricula and provide a higher level of course satisfaction by students.

This compilation of *Current Topics in Technology* is designed to elevate courses in technology to challenge and divert students to develop a higher level cognitive ability that will parallel social, legal, and ethical awareness in the study of technology. Students are guided through a wealth of topics that provide insight into the crucial role that technology occupies in both the personal and professional lives of managers of all organizations. Students will explore their role and responsibilities to the environment and society to ensure that productivity and technical risks are appropriately managed, preparing students for the challenges of leadership. The systematic exercise of the perusal, analysis, and recitation of multiple topics throughout the course will compel students to pursue the content and edification of future topics autonomously. When utilized as part of the critical methods of instruction in introductory courses, the literature and exercises have proven to inspire a greater interest in technology education.

Critical Pedagogy

Students are provided an article overview that serves to introduce the technology topic, providing key background information, which will provide the social, historical, or antecedent events necessary to understand the topic. Following the article, critical thinking questions are provided to stimulate intellectual discussions regarding particular social, political, and ethical values, such as privacy, ownership, crime, responsibility, and risk, while concomitantly reinforcing technical concepts.

Most topics are approached as a mini-case study, similar to the Harvard Business School's practice of detailing an account of a real-life situation in which a dilemma that takes place in a real-life organization is described. This material is utilized most effectively when students read the article and complete the answers to questions individually in writing before meeting in collaborative teams, utilizing the campus extranet system for use of the asynchronous discussion board. Students are motivated by the contrasting perspectives and aliases they share with each other. Following this segue, the discussion is approached in the physical or electronic classroom, using the instructor as the facilitator of the forum. Finally, students are encouraged to participate in scholarly research on topics that emanate from the discussion.

Acknowledgements

The authors extend their appreciation to the Information Technology students and members of the faculty of the Software Engineering Department and School of Business Administration at Monmouth University, for their role in inspiring this effort. Many members of the Information Technology faculty, in particular, made numerous recommendations for articles of interest.

Special recognition is extended to Colleen Sheehan Paparella as a contributing author. Colleen is on the faculty at Oak Knoll School of the Holy Child in Summit, New Jersey, also serving as a college admissions counselor. In addition to an industry position as a reading content developer in St. Louis, Missouri, Colleen is a former New York City Teaching Fellow and has taught full time in New York City Public Schools at the high school and junior high levels. She held positions in the Admissions Departments at two doctoral universities, including Stevens Institute of Technology in Hoboken, New Jersey. She holds a Bachelor of Arts degree with Honors in English and Legal Studies from Washington University in St. Louis and a Master of Science degree in Teaching with a concentration in English from Fordham University.

About the Authors

Maureen Sheehan Paparella and Gene Simko have collaborated on a multitude of research efforts over the last decade in technology education and management of information systems. Their most recent accomplishments include having been inducted as members of Upsilon Pi Epsilon, the International Honor Society of Computing and Information Disciplines, in November of 2008. Eligibility is based upon achievements as denoted by degrees, rank, publications, and high standards of scholarship.

Their most recent research on a new generation of electronic reader technology was featured on the front page of *The Asbury Park Press*, a Gannett newspaper serving Monmouth and Ocean Counties in New Jersey, on February 23, 2009. They presented their research at the University of Northern Virginia-Prague in Prague, Czech Republic, upon acceptance for publication at an international conference in 2008. Also in 2008, two research efforts were accepted for *ICIE Journal* publication (Volume 22), *The Implementation of an Extended Abstract and Multi-Structural Approach to Teaching and Learning Technology* and the *Research Proposal for a Comparative Analysis of Information Technology Education in China and the United States*; the studies were presented at the University of International Business and Economics in Beijing, China in 2007.

Paparella and Simko are also accomplished in the implementation of industrial SWOT analysis, having served most recently as consultants to the Women's Center at Monmouth Medical Center, in Long Branch, New Jersey, in 2009, and in technical management in government, having served as consultants to the Federal Bureau of Investigation at Fort Monmouth, New Jersey, and at headquarters in Washington, D.C. in 2005.

Maureen Sheehan Paparella, the primary author, earned a Bachelor of Arts degree, magna cum laude, from St. Thomas University, Miami, Florida, and earned a Master of Business Administration degree from Barry University, Miami, Florida, where she later taught undergraduate and graduate courses in computer science and developed new curricula in accounting information systems. As a pioneer in the microcomputer industry, Professor Paparella was a software trainer for Texas Instruments, Inc.; she directed microcomputer product support for South Florida, supervising a staff of management trainers and conducting research for the Consumer Products Division and directing technology  education programs for the Education Division. She served as the General Manager of a dealership that provided technology solutions to the South Florida legal market for Sony Corporation of America. Professor Paparella joined the faculty of the Computer Science Department at Monmouth University in 1994, and was appointed Director of Information Technology for the Software Engineering Department in 1997, where she has authored and implemented an Information Technology Minor and Certificate Program, specifically designed for non-technology majors, and a Teacher Computer Camp for K-12 educators. In 2003, she was chosen as one of the first recipients of the Stafford Award for Administrative Excellence. In 2006, she was appointed to the Board of Directors of the International Council for Innovation in Higher Education.

Eugene Simko attended the United States Military Academy at West Point, earned a Bachelor of Science degree and a Master of Business Administration degree from Temple University, Philadelphia, Pennsylvania, and a Doctorate of Strategic Management from Baruch College of the City University of New York. Dr. Simko has consulted for a wide array of organizations in both the public and private sectors, including AT&T, Ralston Purina, Northern Telecom, National Association of Purchasing Managers, Reed Jewelers, Tethered Communications, Bell Northern Research, Mitel, New Jersey Natural Gas, and the American Management Association. He recently served as Acting President of the International Council for Innovation in Higher Education. Dr. Simko is a commissioned officer in the U.S. Army Reserves; served on the New Jersey Assembly Task Force on Business Retention, Expansion and Export Opportunities; and was appointed by the Governor of New Jersey to the New Jersey Battleship Commission. Dr. Simko is a member of the graduate faculty of the Department of Management and Marketing at Monmouth University, has served in numerous administrative posts, such as Associate Provost, Director of Graduate Students, Director of the MBA program, and Vice President of the Faculty Association. Dr. Simko is a recipient of the Monmouth University Distinguished Teaching Award.

FORUM 1
Emerging Technologies and Cyber Exploits

So where were you on February 17th, 2009? It is a global custom to note your place in the world on momentous days in history. Although many legislators supported changing the date itself, the crux of this digital rite of passage is what some naysayers have suggested is U.S. Congressional propaganda! It has been reported that almost $2 billion was spent to prepare citizens technically, with millions more spent by consumers on upgraded equipment. Finally, $1.2 billion was appropriated for a program that included a televised campaign that used the three most important factors in advertising: repetition, repetition, and repetition (Hart and Whoriskey, 2009).

> *"At midnight on February 17th, 2009, all full-power television stations in the United States will stop broadcasting in analog and switch to 100% digital broadcasting. Digital broadcasting promises to provide a clearer picture...and will free up airwaves for use by emergency responders."*

(http://fjallfoss.fcc.gov/edocs_public/attachmatch/FCC-07-228A1.txt)

Digital elitists reminded citizens that most television stations are already broadcasting digitally. For many, this day would be like any other. Joining several other countries that have moved to digital broadcasting, world citizens may learn more practical lessons regarding the transition from analog to digital technology than they ever wanted to know. Some marketers believe this may have a positive impact on consumer electronic sales. The rationale holds that if some customers choose to purchase a new television rather than use the converter box that is provided free of charge, the next logical question is whether consumers will be satisfied with the video capabilities of their other analog equipment, such as VCRs, DVD players, camcorders, gaming consoles, etc. Why? Anecdotally, we have found that even our digital native students infer that "digital" is better than "analog."

Globally, it appears that the digital revolution is most apparent in the conversion from analog landline telephone service to the digital Voice over Internet Protocol (VoIP), the transmission of the human voice over the Internet. By 2011 it is expected that among the 100 million mobile VoIP users worldwide, 33.2 million will be Americans, reflecting 20% annual growth in the number of users in the U.S. (Warburton, 2008).

These are staggering stats in light of VoIP's challenging past, as not very long ago, only extreme competitive pricing could entice most consumers to adopt the service, since a better quality of service already existed in analog form. Yes, once upon a time, it was analog that was deemed better. If you are old enough to recall a dial-up connection via modem as the only choice for most consumers, you surely understand that it was as slow as molasses, resulting in very poor voice quality.

With the use of appropriate software, such as *Microsoft Unified Communications*, voicemail can actually share the same inbox as email, faxes, and calendar events. Imagine never needing to check your voicemail from your phone again because VoIP customers can open their email software and find their voicemail in text. They can save all related text files, the "Smith" account's voicemail messages, and the email "Smith" sent, all to the same folder.

Just as vulnerable to exploitation as other digital technologies, security is a critical factor for VoIP. In fact, perhaps the most obvious sign of its impressive recent growth is that a malicious cyber attack now bears its name. Combining "voice" and "phishing," cyber thieves are now "vishing" (Komando, 2008). Consumers are incredulous to learn that VoIP providers still allow would-be-criminals to enter a caller ID phone number without verification. When consumers see Bank of America's number on the caller ID, for example, are they cognizant that it could be a criminal instead? Don't most consumers trust that the number that appears on a caller ID is, in fact, the number of the caller? This security concern is also referred to as Voice Spam, or SPIT.

You may recall that in the Mumbai, India terror attack in 2008, gunmen called VoIP phone numbers in order to make it harder for law enforcement to trace them. Indeed, the perpetrators used this technology to gain a tactical advantage (Wax, 2008).

As is often the case with the use of new technology, legislative action is lagging. A bill initiated in 2007 resides in the U.S. Congressional Truth in Caller ID Act of 2009 introduced in March of 2009. (http://www.opencongress.org/bill/111-h1258/show). Thus, hope for a solution is on the frontier.

Other security concerns include toll fraud, the theft of long distance services, and Brute Force, an attempt to bypass a security check or determine a password by attempting possible options until finding one that works. Eavesdropping on data packets also makes it possible to determine passwords as well as confidential company business. VoIP networks are particularly vulnerable to Denial of Service (DoS) Attacks and Distributed Denial of Service Attacks, and overwhelming the network and bringing it down can result in prolonged busy signals (Blake, 2007).

While vishing might be classified as a *remote* exploit because it exploits the security vulnerability without any prior access to the system, Denial of Service may be classified as a *superuser* exploit. Jonathan Yarden of *TechRepublic* reminds us that "when attackers take advantage of an exploit, one of their first goals" is to gain administrator, or superuser, access to the compromised system (Yarden, 2004). A new iteration of an old program called *Coreflood* is a superuser exploit that began in 2001 and is said to have been reiterated more than 100 times.

The *Coreflood* Trojan records keystrokes and captures screen information, including passwords. In its most current iteration, it has proven the ability to attack a system administrator's machine, and then use the administrator's privileges to infect all other machines within the administrator's domain. By attacking just one machine, it has the ability to infect tens of thousands more machines in a matter of a few hours.

Benjamin Franklin is noted as writing, "In this world, nothing is certain but death and taxes" (Bartlett, 1919). Surely if Franklin were alive today, he may have considered adding one more life certainty: nothing is certain but death, taxes, and security exploits.

Article: Russian Gang Hijacking PCs in Vast Scheme

By John Markoff
August 5, 2008
The New York Times

A criminal gang is using software tools normally reserved for computer network administrators to infect thousands of PCs in corporate and government networks with programs that steal passwords and other information, a security researcher has found.

The new form of attack indicates that little progress has been made in defusing the threat of botnets, networks of infected computers that criminals use to send spam, steal passwords and do other forms of damage, according to computer security investigators.

Several security experts say that although attacks against network administrators are not new, the systematic use of administrative software to spread malicious software has not been widely seen until now.

The gang was identified publicly in May by Joe Stewart, director of malware research at SecureWorks, a computer security firm in Atlanta. Mr. Stewart, who has determined that the gang is based in Russia, was able to locate a central program controlling as many as 100,000 infected computers across the Internet. The program was running at a commercial Internet hosting computer center in Wisconsin.

Mr. Stewart alerted a federal law enforcement agency that he declined to identify, and he said that it was investigating the matter. Although the original command program was shut down, the gang immediately reconstituted the system, he said, moving the control program to another computer in the Ukraine, beyond the reach of law enforcement in the United States.

The system infects PCs with a program known as Coreflood that records keystrokes and steals other information. The network of infected computers collected as much as 500 gigabytes of data in a little more than a year and sent it back to the Wisconsin computer center, Mr. Stewart said.

One of the unique aspects of the malicious software is that it captures screen information in addition to passwords, according to Mark Seiden, a veteran computer security engineer. That makes it possible for gang members to see information like bank balances without having to log in to stolen accounts.

Mr. Stewart's discoveries are evidence that while the botnet problem is now well understood, botnets are still a widespread threat.

"The rate of infection is still high, but concern among corporations is low," said Rick Wesson, a botnet investigator at Support Intelligence, a security consulting firm in San Francisco. "Many corporations seem to think it's O.K. to be infected several times a month."

Mr. Stewart and other computer security investigators have previously described the activities of the gang that uses the Coreflood program. But Mr. Stewart plans to offer new details about the gang, which has operated with impunity for several years, at the Black Hat Briefings computer security conference that begins Thursday in Las Vegas.

As part of his investigation, Mr. Stewart charted the rate of computer infections at a state police agency and a large hotel chain. Both were victims of an outbreak that began after the gang obtained the password and login information of their network administrators. In both cases hundreds or thousands of computers were infected within minutes or hours.

Mr. Stewart would not name the organizations because of the continuing law enforcement investigation.

In these examples as well as a range of others, the gang infected a machine belonging to an administrator and then used Microsoft administrative tools to infect all the computers for which that person had responsibility, Mr. Stewart said.

The new attack is a byproduct of the way modern computer networks are administered, where authority is centralized and software updates for thousands of machines are automated.

"The great thing about this system is that from one computer it is possible to push out updates to all machines in a corporate network at once," Mr. Stewart said. "This is a useful tool that Microsoft has provided. However, the bad guys said, 'We'll just use it to roll out our Trojan to every machine in the network.' "

A Microsoft spokesman declined to comment on the attacks.

Mr. Stewart said that the gang behind the Coreflood program was responsible for 378,000 infections over 16 months. In each case the infected computer would capture and transmit personal information to a centralized database that kept track of the "spies" in the network.

In his Black Hat presentation, Mr. Stewart plans to say that he believes the Russian gang was behind a successful theft of money from the bank account of a Miami businessman, Joe Lopez.

In April 2004, someone made an unauthorized wire transfer of $90,348 from Mr. Lopez's account with Bank of America to Parex Bank in Riga, Latvia. Of that amount, $20,000 was successfully withdrawn by a person using a false identity. The Coreflood program was found on Mr. Lopez's computer.

After discovering the control program in Wisconsin, Mr. Stewart tracked the online activities of some gang members in a Russian city that he declined to identify because of the investigation.

He said translations of some entries on the blogging site LiveJournal had led him to believe that one member of the gang had died, but that others remained active. He said that he had provided investigators with a wealth of information about the group from members' online discussions and other material he had collected.

"If the Russians are sincerely interested in tracking these guys down, I think it's possible," he said.

Things to Think About

1. "Visual collaboration" is the joining of two or more individuals to use a combination of audio, video, and data streams, all merged into a seamless infrastructure and now available in most markets. Would the use of video in VoIP serve to protect users from vishing exploits?

2. Explain the difference between a security vulnerability and an exploit.

3. Is VoIP subject to the same sorts of attacks as data networks configured for the Internet, including Denial of Service Attacks? Explain.

4. Why might you expect that fax calls, security alarm systems, and modems would not work reliably over the same network used for VoIP?

5. Explain how the Coreflood Trojan causes damage and what precautionary measures can be implemented.

Key Terms

1. Vishing

2. Trojan

FORUM 2
Cybercriminal Profiling

I n the early 1980s, much of the population of the United States was concerned about surviving an economic recession, as mortgage rates escalated beyond 16% (FDIC.gov, 2005).

But there were other causes of anxiety for many. While this was an exciting and momentous time in technology history, as computers were now available to the masses for the very first time, the enormous change to the workplace served to coin a new category of employee, the "computer phobic." Many feared that this new machine would serve to replace jobs and the personal pleasures of working with humans. The use of the computer was so foreign and appeared so complicated that anyone who could use it successfully was usually regarded as intellectually gifted.

There was one group of mostly male persons at that time, however, who had no fear of this new machine. They strongly bonded to each other due to their shared enthusiasm for using the computer. Their profile could be best described as task-oriented, junk-food nourished, introverted within social circles outside their shared interests in computers, yet brilliant for having figured out how to use this machine to solve problems. In addition, they were naturally nocturnal, preferring the distraction-free timelessness of the night to reach deep levels of concentration as they worked. Their personal commitment was to dismantle barriers to information and communication established by a market culture. These young men were driven not by profits, but by a passion for their "ethic of information sharing." Their work provided an outlet for entertainment, socialization, and professional growth, and their worlds avoided authority, hierarchy, and rules. We affectionately called these individuals *hackers*. (The Modus Operandi of Hacking: Sociological Perspective-http://www.apsu.edu/oconnort/3100/3100lect02a.htm).

Actually, a few of their names may be familiar to you. Steve Jobs, handsome and poised on stage, was born to a young unwed graduate student, who so loved her son that she was determined to locate college-degreed adoptive parents who could afford to send him to college. The highly educated chosen couple suddenly changed their minds at the time of Jobs' birth in favor of adopting a girl. A new couple, who did not meet the degree requirements, wanted this baby boy so much that they begged his biological mother to allow them to be his parents and promised to send him to college. Jobs, in turn, so loved his parents that soon after arriving at college, he decided to drop out as a full-time student and refrain from spending their hard-earned life savings to complete often unsatisfying courses at Reed College. In order to save money, he often slept on the floors of his friends' dorm rooms and took only the most interesting courses, such as a calligraphy course that inspired him to design the stellar typeface capabilities of his computer 10 years later. Jobs told this story to Stanford graduates in 2005, reminding them of how connecting the dots on our life paths may provide us the confidence to accept detours. Jobs befriended another young man of his ilk named Steve Wozniak, who dropped out of

Berkeley to build computers with Jobs. In fact, together they founded Apple Computer in 1976 (Stanford, 2005).

You may also have heard of a man named Bill Gates. When Gates was in eighth grade, his best buddy was Paul Allen; they shared a strong interest in developing programs for computers. This was during an era in which users did not own personal computers, but rather were required to pay for the time they consumed on a computer. Gates and Allen quickly became efficient in detecting security vulnerabilities that allowed them to exploit the computer their school had purchased time on in order to acquire more usage time. In fact, they were banned from using the computer for the summer when they were caught. Later, the company providing computer time to the school used the talents of Gates and Allen to assist them. Much later, Gates dropped out of Harvard and Allen dropped out of Washington State in order to pursue *soft*ware development for *micro*computers, creating a new firm named *Micro-soft* (Ramana, 2008).

Do you notice a pattern in the lives of these men? All levels of government, education, and industry are particularly interested in the profile of hackers and many have just recently realized that the profile of hackers has changed significantly. Jobs, Wozniak, Gates, and Allen were all college dropouts who were gifted intellectually and passionate about creating computer systems. (Wozniak did later return to earn his college degree.) Combined with a healthy bit of rebellion, they even may have found themselves involved in breaking the law in their youth. Industry and government often utilized their skills in positive ways in the aftermath and everyone involved appeared to have lived happily every after, making enormous contributions to society, and reaping vast benefits.

Thus, "hacker" began as a term that was synonymous with "nerd." In fact, urban legend asserts that Bill Gates even developed a list of commandments for students, one of which reminds them to be nice to "nerds," because "some day you will probably be working for one." It was a notion that no one doubted (Snopes.com reports that the correct source for the commandments is Charles Sykes of the *San Diego Union Tribune, Some Rules Kids Won't Learn in School*, September 19, 1996).

Today, the term "hacker" describes a person of an entirely different genre. It refers to a cybercriminal driven by narcissism, greed, and destruction.

Article: Hackers' mind-set: They've done nothing wrong

By Jon Swartz
October 23, 2008
USA Today

SAN FRANCISCO—Albert Gonzalez appeared to be a reformed hacker. But the onetime government informant was a central character in what Justice Department officials claim was an international cybercrime syndicate that ripped off tens of millions of credit and debit card numbers from large U.S. retailers.

Irving Jose Escobar seemed nothing more than a tough Miami kid with a long rap sheet. Yet last year, he pleaded guilty to his role in a multimillion-dollar scam in Florida tied to Gonzalez's exploit.

What they shared, based on indictments in their separate cases, are key roles in the massive cyberheist at TJX, parent of retailers T.J. Maxx and Marshalls, and the credit card scams that resulted. First disclosed by TJX in January 2007, it is believed to be the largest such theft.

It is unclear whether Gonzalez and Escobar know each other. But each was involved in different scams tied to TJX, according to their respective indictments. The divergent sagas of the hacker Gonzalez and streetwise Escobar represent bookends of the vast digital crime. According to psychiatrists, hackers and computer-security experts, they represent the vanguard of cybercrooks: young, misguided males who rationalize that they've done nothing wrong.

Like Escobar and Gonzalez, many are adamant they are innocent. "These are rattlesnakes without the rattles," says Greg Saathoff, a psychiatry professor at the University of Virginia who is one of the world's foremost profilers of criminals. "The movie portrayal is they are evil geniuses who are absolutely controlling and calculated, but they can be impulsive and grandiose."

A 27-year-old Cuban American, Gonzalez had been arrested in 2003 on credit card fraud charges in New Jersey and agreed to cooperate with authorities to avoid jail time. According to the Secret Service, Gonzalez helped agents infiltrate Shadowcrew, an online ring of credit card thieves.

But that didn't stop him from later heading a ring that stole more than 40 million credit and debit card numbers from TJX and eight other major U.S. retailers, according to a federal indictment. He faces life in prison if convicted on charges of computer fraud, wire fraud, access-device fraud, aggravated identity theft and conspiracy, a Justice spokeswoman says. Gonzalez pleaded not guilty at a Sept. 11 arraignment in a Boston federal court.

Through his digital crime spree, according to the indictment, Gonzalez amassed more than $1.65 million—including about $22,500 in cash—a condo in Miami, a BMW 330i and a stash of high-tech equipment, including laptops and a cellphone.

Some of the stolen TJX data were magnetically encoded on bogus credit cards and eventually made their way to Escobar, convicted last year on charges of credit card fraud. Escobar led a group of six street-level "mules" in Florida that included his wife and mother, according to a criminal complaint by the Florida Department of Law Enforcement. They took the plastic to Wal-Mart stores in Florida to buy gift cards that could be used like cash. They then used the gift cards to purchase more than $1 million worth of PCs, big-screen TVs, jewelry and other expensive items, state officials said.

Escobar, 20, has steadfastly professed his innocence. In a letter to USA TODAY in July, he said he was eager to offer a rare, first-person account into his experience. He is serving five years in a Florida prison. "There are to (sic) many errors going in my case, things that the secret service agents didn't bring out to the light," Escobar wrote. "The only person that knows all the truth is me, and I'm willing to let it out to the light so society could realize how corrupt it (sic) this world we're living in."

But shortly before a scheduled prison interview at the Brevard Correctional Institution in Cocoa, Fla., Escobar abruptly declined.

Profile of cybercriminals

Many cybercrooks are young men in the U.S. and Eastern Europe who think they're doing the system a favor by exposing flaws and have no qualms about opportunities to exploit rich Westerners, according to police, researchers and hackers.

Their motivation is "money, money, money," says Dan Kaminsky, director of penetration testing for security firm IOActive, who in July discovered a huge vulnerability in the Internet's design that lets cybercrooks silently redirect traffic to websites under their control.

Most hackers do not see themselves as criminals, says David Perry, who as global director of education at computer-security giant Trend Micro has interviewed cybercrooks for more than a decade. "They simply believe they are showing vulnerabilities in the system."

The TJX cell's loose confederation of individuals—each contributed a unique felonious skill from different parts of the world—is a blueprint for organized crime in the digital age, says Mark Rasch, a former Justice Department cybercrime prosecutor.

Federal prosecutors portray the 6-foot, 190-pound Gonzalez as the chief organizer in the TJX case, a charge his attorney, Rene Palomino, disputes.

Gonzalez is a self-taught computer consultant who first met several of the other defendants online, says Palomino, who says the charges against his client have stunned Gonzalez's parents in Miami.

"This is a hardworking, churchgoing family," he says. "There is a lot of so-called evidence from people trying to wash off their bad acts. When the truth surfaces, it will surprise a lot of people, including the government."

The Justice Department alleges that in 2003, Gonzalez began hacking the computer networks of TJX, BJ's Wholesale Club, OfficeMax, Boston Market, Barnes & Noble, Sports Authority, Forever 21, DSW and Dave & Buster's.

Millions of stolen credit and debit card numbers were allegedly stored on computer servers in the United States, Latvia and Ukraine. The stolen data were sold, via the Internet, to other criminals in the U.S. and Eastern Europe, the indictment says.

Escobar's criminal endeavor was a family affair.

His wife, Zenia Llorente, 25, got probation for fraud for her part in the scam. His mother, Nair Zuleima Alvarez, 42, was given a jail sentence for fraud and later deported to her native Venezuela last year, says John Wethington, assistant prosecutor for Florida Attorney General Bill McCollum.

The 5-foot-10, 211-pound Escobar, who was sentenced to five years in prison and faces deportation to Venezuela upon his scheduled release in 2012, has maintained he is a victim of a corrupt system.

Florida court records show Escobar had several scrapes with the law in Miami-Dade County before he was busted for his role in TJX. From 2003 to 2007, Escobar was charged at least eight times, the charges ranging from "home-invasion robbery" to illegal use of a credit card. Those charges were dropped or abandoned. He was arrested and charged with cocaine possession and placed in a drug-diversion program in 2007.

"To this day, he thinks he is the only victim," says Amy Osteryoung, the former Florida assistant prosecutor in charge of Escobar's case.

"The thousands and thousands of people who had their personal information stolen were just collateral damage to him."

Things to Think About

1. Describe the massive cyberheist at TJX.

2. Psychologists tell us that the new cybercriminal believes that he or she has done nothing wrong. Do you believe that Bill Gates and Paul Allen believed the same when they took additional computer time without paying for it? How would you compare their belief systems with that of those involved in TJX?

3. The description of the cybercriminal today includes the adjectives "impulsive" and "grandiose," and includes a strong interest in money. How does this differ from the hacker of the 80s? Describe the new profile and its challenges for law enforcement.

4. Do you believe that the same hacker driven by profit motives is also driven by an interest in exposing network vulnerabilities? In what category of cybercriminal would you place Albert Gonzalez and Irving Jose Escobar? Explain.

5. Describe a mule. Is it possible that the mules were unaware of the part they played in the crime?

Key Terms

1. TJX

2. Mule

FORUM 3
Technology Infrastructure:
The "Semantic Web" on Computers with
"Personalities"

Tracy Kidder won a Pulitzer Prize for his best seller, *The Soul of a New Machine*, in which he profiles a small team of computer designers in 1981. The passion exhibited by these pioneers in technology often stems from their realization at the outset that the machine was capable of dramatically changing the way we live, think, and work. Today, having software and hardware available via the Internet, often free and customizable, those changes appear more frequently. Open source software such as the Linux Operating System, OpenOffice.org, Diigo, and Dropbox has proven to be reputable, dependable, and supported. The Web now provides the storage space on hardware that allows consumers to save their files both publicly and privately. Web 2.0, the second generation of the Web, is often referred to as "cloud computing" by marketers because it suggests that we now have the possibility of saving our data "in the cloud" (remote servers), permitting consumers to save as much as 2 gigabytes of data with no charge. A new small business no longer needs to be concerned about purchasing servers or even sending attachments to update files. We no longer need to send documents to others; we go to the documents on the server on the Web.

Now, just 15 years after the Internet became commercially available, we are moving toward using artificial intelligence to create Web 3.0, also referred to as the Semantic Web. Instead of matching a tagged keyword to locate a word in an article, we will expect our browser to truly understand the meaning of the word. If I enter "love" in a typical search box today, for example, I will receive links to sources that include that word. The computer will just blindly retrieve the information based upon syntax, or grammar. If I enter "adore," the Web might not include articles about love because it does not understand that "love" and "adore" are related. Instead, it will only respond with sources that include the word "adore." With a Web that is semantic, we might enter special code within HTML, the language used to create Web pages, that would allow the computer to "understand" word meanings by creating a connection between the two words. Thus, whether we entered "love" or "adore," we might retrieve links to resources that explore love. On a Web that is semantic, users can expect that when the name of a singer is entered, instead of just retrieving all the text found that includes that singer's name, the entire list of songs that singer is noted for singing would also appear. With the Semantic Web, a tool such as Resource Description Framework (RDF) integrates various applications from library catalogs, for example, to a personal collection of music. RDF was developed by the World Wide Web Consortium (W3C). It is an infrastructure that enables the encoding and reuse of structured metadata, the information that characterizes data (http://www.w3.org/RDF).

With greater use of the Web as a place to store our data, the space to store it and the energy to run the supercomputers that form its backbone are also paramount. One of the original designers who endured the technological frontier reported about in Kidder's book, Steve Wallach, has created the ability to warehouse data and process it on a smaller, easier to use, less expensive, faster, and "greener" computer. The *Convey* is a supercomputer in which various "personalities" can be programmed on the hardware. If you remember that a program is simply a list of instructions that tells the computer what to do, imagine if instruction sets were created for a wide array of industries, such as the biomedical industry, and for applications that are very commonly used. These instruction sets are programmed to the hardware device. The *Convey* computer includes a base instruction set as well. Its architects claim that it represents a reduction of 83% in the amount of floor space it uses and an 84% reduction in power cooling, as a result. It uses a new chip technology called *Field Programmable Gate Arrays* that is easily reprogrammed.

So it seems that we are maintaining our files in a "cloud" rather than on our computers, inserting an RDF framework within HTML code when designing our Web sites for better search results, and writing our code to processor chips rather than running them from secondary storage devices.

Article: A Computing Pioneer Has a New Idea

By John Markoff
November 16, 2008
The New York Times

SAN FRANCISCO—Steven J. Wallach is completing the soul of his newest machine.

Thirty years ago, Mr. Wallach was one of a small team of computer designers profiled by Tracy Kidder in his Pulitzer Prize winning best seller, "The Soul of a New Machine."

It was Mr. Wallach, then 33, who served as the architect and baby sitter for his "microkids," the young team that designed the Data General MV 8000, the underdog minicomputer that kept the company alive in its brutal competition with the Digital Equipment Corporation.

At 63, he is still at it. He plans to introduce his new company, Convey Computer, and to describe the technical details of a new supercomputer intended for scientific and engineering applications at a supercomputing conference in Austin, Tex., this week.

Mr. Wallach thinks he has come upon a new idea in computer design in an era when it has become fashionable to say that there are no new ideas. So far, he has persuaded some of the leading thinkers in the high performance computing world that he might be right. Both Intel and a second chip maker, Xilinx, have joined as early investors.

"Steve comes from a long history of building successful machines," said Jack Dongarra, a computer scientist at the University of Tennessee who helps maintain the list of the world's fastest 500 computers. "He understands where the bottlenecks are."

After leaving Data General, Mr. Wallach helped found Convex in 1982 to build a low-cost supercomputer.

Mr. Wallach may be one of the few people remaining to recall a bold generation of computer designers once defined by Seymour Cray, the engineer who created the world's first commercial supercomputers during the 1960s.

His newest effort in computing design is intended to tackle one of the principal limitations in the world of supercomputing. Typically supercomputers are intended to excel in solving a single class of problems. They may simulate the explosion of a nuclear weapon or model global climate change at blinding speed, but for other problems they will prove sluggish and inefficient.

Today's supercomputers are assembled from thousands or even tens of thousands of microprocessors, and they often consume as much electricity as a small city. Moreover, they can prove to be frightfully difficult to program. Many new supercomputers try to deal with the challenge of solving different classes of problems by connecting different kinds of processors together Lego-style. This can give programmers fits.

For decades, computer designers have struggled with different ways to sidestep the complexity of programming multiple chips, in order to break up problems into pieces to be computed simultaneously so that they can be solved more quickly.

Mr. Wallach came up with his new design idea in 2006 after he found himself rejecting many of the start-up companies who were coming to the venture capital companies he was advising.

"I would say, 'No, no, no, they're clueless,' " he said. "I find it difficult to think of myself as the old man of the industry, but it feels the same as it was in the early 1980s."

One of the venture capitalists grew frustrated with Mr. Wallach's repeated criticisms and said to him, "All right Mr. Bigshot, what would you do?"

Two weeks later, Mr. Wallach had a new idea. He had long been fascinated with a chip technology called Field Programmable Gate Arrays. These chips are widely used to make prototype computer systems because they can be easily reprogrammed and yet offer the pure speed of computer hardware. There have been a number of start-ups and large supercomputer companies that have already tried to design systems based on the chips, but Mr. Wallach thought that he could do a better job.

The right way to use them, he decided, was to couple them so tightly to the microprocessor chip that it would appear they were simply a small set of additional instructions to give a programmer an easy way to turbocharge a program. Everything had to look exactly like the standard programming environment. In contrast, many supercomputers today require programmers to be "heroic."

"The past 40 years has taught us that ultimately the system that is easiest to program will always win," he said.

Mr. Wallach approached Advanced Micro Devices about partnering, but it was skeptical. So he went to Intel, where he knew Justin Rattner, the company's chief technology officer and a veteran supercomputer designer.

"We've had enough debates over the years that Justin has some respect for me," he said.

The Convey computer will be based around Intel's microprocessors. It will perform like a shape-shifter, reconfiguring with different hardware "personalities" to compute problems for different industries, initially aiming at bioinformatics, computer-aided design, financial services and oil and gas exploration.

Mr. Wallach acknowledges that starting a company going into a recession in the face of stiff competition from Cray, I.B.M., Hewlett-Packard, Sun Microsystems and more than a dozen smaller companies is daunting. However, Convey was put together in just two years on a shoestring. It has raised just $15.1 million.

"In a lot of ways, it's easier than it was in 1982," he said. "You need less money and I don't think a lot of people have grasped this."

One who does get the idea and who is enthusiastic about it is Larry Smarr, an astrophysicist who is director of the California Institute for Telecommunications and Information Technology at the University of California, San Diego. He believes that the most important quality of the Convey computer is that it will be a green supercomputer.

"The I.T. industry is going to become the boogeyman for global warming," he worries.

Three decades after designing the computer that brought the idea of computing into the public consciousness, Mr. Wallach gives no hint that he is slowing down.

He still wears the earring that he began wearing 15 years ago when his daughter suggested that he was getting old.

"Isn't that required to be a computer architect?" he asked recently.

Things to Think About

1. How will a Semantic Web change the way we use the Web?

2. What are the potential risks of moving in the direction of the Semantic Web?

3. Does the Convey represent a new generation of supercomputers? Explain.

4. Explain how the first and second generations of the Web differ from the Semantic Web. Explain the numbering system, 1.0, 2.0, and 3.0.

5. Explain the use of the term "personalities" on the Convey computer.

Key Terms

1. Semantic Web

2. RDF

FORUM 4
Internet Violence and Cyber Safety

"There is nothing sacrosanct about the Internet," stated Australian National University ethics professor, Clive Hamilton (Foley, 2008). "We live in a society, and societies have always imposed limits…" Hamilton's frustrations were apparent as he defended his nation's $82 million "cyber safety plan." Scheduled to be in place in May 2009, it is intended to protect children online by restricting access to child pornography and materials related to terrorism. But what Hamilton calls "a victory for common sense," libertarians decry as a serious violation of free speech, as they band together in social Web site communities to plan protests. There have been many attempts to deal with the issues of violence, pornography, and privacy on the Internet, giving rise to the inevitable tension between free speech and safety.

That there are serious consequences for young people is well documented. In the case of *Roper v. Simmons*, the American Medical Association writes in the *Amicus Brief* to the Supreme Court, "The adolescent mind works differently than ours…Their brains are physiologically underdeveloped in the areas that control impulses, foresee consequences and temper emotions…The insight emerges from sophisticated and noninvasive brain imaging techniques" (U.S. Supreme Court, 2005).

Almost every/day, new reports surface that attest to these findings. One such case involved a Missouri teen, Megan Meier, who committed suicide after suffering relentless harassment by an Internet imposter.

Jessie, 18, sent her boyfriend an intimate picture of herself, now referred to as "sexting." When they broke up, he then impulsively passed it on to her high school peers. After persistent verbal abuse from her classmates, Jessica, in the midst of depression, also took her life (Celizic, 2009).

In January of 2009, three young ladies were charged with "manufacturing, disseminating, and possessing" child pornography when they sent nude photos of themselves to male classmates (Brunker, 2009).

After his former girlfriend mistreated him, Philip, 18, opted for revenge by electronically blasting the nude photos she once sent him to 70 people, including her parents and teachers. Philip was charged with transmitting child pornography and is registered as a sex offender as he serves five years of probation (Prieto, 2009).

The New York Times reports that "digital dating violence" and "textual abuse" very often begin with a constant flow of emails, recognized as a means to control its victim. Now, a public service campaign organized by the Advertising Council highlights awareness of this escalating problem by supplying "callout cards" for victims to send to perpetrators from its Web site, *ThatsNotCool.com* (Clifford, 2009). Because of similar findings online, tech.blorge.com reports that the European Commission has negotiated agreements with MySpace, Facebook, and 17 other social networking sites to set the default configurations of the profiles and contact lists of minors to private. In addition, their accounts will be hidden from searches, both on the sites and from external search engines (Meller, 2009).

Perhaps the most scandalous news we learned in this investigation on Internet violence was the existence of a new video game available for purchase over the Internet, which appeared to espouse that which most social scientists consider one of the most extreme forms of violence. A Japan-based firm distributed a virtual-rape game. Players stalk and sexually assault mothers and daughters and much more. It was pulled by Amazon upon the outrage of one of its bloggers. Paradoxically, a spokesman for the firm, *Illusion*, claimed it has cleared the domestic ratings of an ethics watchdog body (*Fox News*, 2009).

"We will see that cyberspace does not guarantee its own freedom, but instead carries an extraordinary potential for control," the Internet law expert Lawrence Lessig stated in his famous book, *Code and Other Laws of Cyberspace* (Basic Books, 2006). Lessig reminds us that "when government disappears, it is not as if paradise will take its place" (Lessig, 2006).

In the United States there has been limited legislation directed toward this end. The most recent legislation is the Broadband Data Improvement Act, signed into law in 2008. Although much of the law is focused on increased reporting, it also requires the Federal Trade Commission to develop an Internet Safety campaign for children. In 1998, the United States Child Online Protection Act (COPA) restricted access to "material harmful to minors" on the Internet by imposing penalties on those posting content on the Web. By 2004, however, the United States Supreme Court agreed with a lower court ruling that COPA was likely to be found unconstitutional on the grounds that it violated the First Amendment rights of adults. Instead, the court focused on voluntary blocking and filtering software programs at the receiving end rather than universal restrictions on the source. In addition, the courts cited pragmatic reasons such as the inability for a law to prevent access to foreign sites that would hold harmful material. The U.S. courts did impose the Children's Online Privacy Protection Act (COPPA), executed in 2000, which is directed at Web sites used for commercial purposes and requires parental consent in order to use and collect data on children under 13 years old.

Lessig reminds us that it may be time for "real space" legal values to arrive in "cyberspace" (Lessig, 2006).

Article: YouTube Bans Videos That Incite Violence

By Peter Whoriskey
September 12, 2008
The Washington Post

The video-sharing service YouTube is banning submissions that involve "inciting others to violence," following criticism from Sen. Joseph I. Lieberman (I-Conn.) that the site was too open to terrorist groups disseminating militant propaganda.

The company earlier this year removed some of the videos that Lieberman targeted, many of which were marked with the logos of al-Qaeda and affiliated groups. But the company refused to take down most of the videos on the senator's list, saying they did not violate the Web site's guidelines against graphic violence or hate speech.

Now that videos inciting others to violence are banned, more videos by the terrorist groups in question may be removed.

"YouTube reviews its content guidelines a few times a year, and we take the community's input seriously," YouTube spokesman Ricardo Reyes said. "The senator made some good points."

"YouTube was being used by Islamist terrorist organizations to recruit and train followers via the Internet and to incite terrorist attacks around the world, including right here in the United States," Lieberman said in a statement. "I expect these stronger community guidelines to decrease the number of videos on YouTube produced by al-Qaeda and affiliated Islamist terrorist organizations."

The standoff between the senator and the nation's largest video-sharing site aroused arguments that have become commonplace since Sept. 11, 2001: It pitted civil rights—in this case, free speech—against demands to crack down on terrorism.

In May, Lieberman issued a bipartisan report by the Senate Committee on Homeland Security and Governmental Affairs staff that described how al-Qaeda created and managed its online media.

Later that month, Lieberman wrote a letter to officials at Google [which owns YouTube] demanding that the company "immediately remove content produced by Islamic terrorist organizations from YouTube. This should be a straightforward task since so many of the Islamist terrorist organizations brand their material with logos or icons."

He also asked Google to explain what changes would be made to YouTube's guidelines to address "violent extremist material."

Because the volume of videos uploaded to YouTube is vast—hundreds of thousands every day—the company says it cannot monitor what gets posted. Instead, it relies on users to flag videos that violate its "Community Guidelines."

When the company removed videos after Lieberman's request in May, the company did so because they violated its existing guidelines prohibiting graphic violence and hate speech. Some of the videos depicted violent attacks on U.S. soldiers in Iraq and Afghanistan.

But most of the videos highlighted by Lieberman were not removed.

"While we respect and understand his [Lieberman's] views, YouTube encourages free speech and defends everyone's right to express unpopular points of view," the company said in a statement at the time.

The company's stance now appears to have changed.

Exactly what kind of videos will be deemed to be "inciting others to violence," will be considered on a case-by-case basis, though First Amendment experts said the company could run into trouble if the phrase is interpreted too broadly.

"We subscribe to the common sense rule," Reyes said. "Our guidelines are not written for lawyers."

Things to Think About

1. Do you view the Web as a community of people, or rather, as a place of "code," as Lessig seems to suggest?

2. Prof. Hamilton suggests that libertarians view the Internet as "sacrosanct." What do you think of this notion of the Internet as free from government regulation?

3. YouTube refers to "common sense" decision making in the removal of videos. Could it be that our sense of what is common, or acceptable, is different, depending upon the mores of the society in which we live? Explain.

4. Google, the firm that owns YouTube, reported revenues of $21.8 billion in 2008 with net income at $4.23 billion. How would you make the financial case for hiring an additional thousand employees for the sole purpose of monitoring video uploads?

5. Could the Terrorism Act of 2006 force YouTube to remove material that is illegal if watched by the British?

Key Terms

1. Terrorism Act of 2006

2. Callout cards

FORUM 5
Educational Technology and Compliance

Perhaps one of the greatest challenges for educational administrators over the previous decade was to communicate to legislators that the implementation of No Child Left Behind (NCLB) required funding that was not readily available. More recently, for higher education, adhering to the directives of the Higher Education Opportunity Act has heightened a similar awareness, and for many, an ethical responsibility to advocate for their students. With already constrained budgets, how will higher education absorb the costs associated with enforcement of laws to stem digital piracy?

According to the Institute for Policy Innovation, the music industry loses $12.5 billion a year worldwide to piracy (Siwek, 2007). Similar to practices in the U.S, where action has been taken against 35,000 violators, Britain has recently required its Internet Service Providers to provide warnings to pirates that their identities will be forwarded to rights holders for possible legal action. But where the U.S. falls short, France will more directly meet the request of rights holders by using a "graduated response" system that first warns customers and then terminates their service from 1 to 12 months. New Zealand, Italy, Hong Kong, Australia, Ireland, and South Korea have made advances in the same direction (Kennedy, 2009). While the RIAA is seeking the same policy in the U.S., it does not appear that plans are on the horizon to meet that request. Instead, it appears that the problem has fallen on the shoulders of higher education and indirectly, students who pay tuition.

Yet currently, an even different point of view arises from the ashes, and it is finding support within the academic community. In light of recent claims made by researchers at the University of Oxford in 2008, it may be a logical expectation of taxpayers to think critically about responding to this burden at all. Dr. Karen Croxson suggests that piracy does not actually undermine profits. Instead, she suggests that pirates may be inadvertently promoting products. She even alludes to other business practices as evidence. Croxson points out that those pirates, as consumers, will talk to other potential customers about their product experiences, a key factor in sales success. Her research supports studies that show that piracy drives up the "buzz" and therefore, reduces marketing costs (*University of Oxford*, 2008).

Doesn't this have a ring of familiarity to it? Our students have been arguing this anecdotally for years!

Article: What Are the Costs of P2P Compliance?

By David Nagel
October 20, 2008
Campus Technology

With the signing into law of the Higher Education Opportunity Act of 2008 back in August, colleges and universities now face the prospect of providing pro-bono enforcement services for the RIAA and MPAA in their efforts to thwart illegal file sharing. What are the costs of these services to individual campuses? According to a new report issued Monday by the Campus Computing Project, the annual direct, technology-related costs alone range from a low of about $29,000 to a high of about $408,000, depending on the type of institution.

The report, "The Campus Costs of P2P Compliance," covers in some detail the background of the new Higher Education Act legislation and its implications for campuses, breaking down expenses by type of expense and staff time committed to enforcement, all by type of campus—public universities, private universities, etc. What it found was that, on the higher end of the spectrum, private universities spent some $407,784 in academic year 2007-2008 on software licenses ($105,126), hardware costs ($158,714), and other direct costs ($143,944) for controlling piracy on their campuses. Public universities came in second, at $169,882 ($22,482 for software, $64,618 for hardware, and $82,782 for other direct costs).

Public and private bachelor's colleges came in with the lowest direct annual IT expenses attributed to P2P compliance efforts, at $38,660 and $29,171, respectively. Other institutions measured included public master's institutions ($55,002 in annual direct expenses), private master's institutions ($48,574), and public associate degree-granting colleges ($58,482).

The research was based on a survey of 321 two- and four-year colleges and universities conducted this summer.

According to the report, "The data from the summer 2008 P2P survey confirm that compliance with the HEA P2P mandates involves significant costs for the nation's colleges and universities. For some large doctoral institutions, these costs—cash and personnel time—easily exceed half a million dollars annually. From one perspective, these campus expenditures seem to be a significant 'enforcement subsidy' that supports the entertainment industry's efforts to stem digital piracy. In the wake of the new HEA legislation, these P2P compliance expenditures are now a mandated subsidy."

The amount of time campus personnel and legal counsel dedicated to P2P issues varied widely by job type and institution type. The report showed that at public universities, the combined mean time spent on P2P issues by IT personnel (ranging from CIOs and IT managers to IT help desk staff and secretarial support and administration) in academic year 2007-2008 was 778.7 hours. Private universities were right up there as well, at a combined mean of 606.6 hours for all IT personnel. And while IT may incur the bulk of the burden of time in these compliance activities, other departments are also impacted, from student affairs to administrators to legal counsel.

And, what's more, both the financial costs and costs in time spent enforcing P2P policies are expected to grow.

"In aggregate and over time," the report said, "there's little question that for most institutions, P2P compliance will consume more dollars from campus budgets and more hours from campus personnel."

Things to Think About

1. What are the economic implications of ignoring enforcement of piracy? Are intangible properties an asset, just as tangible assets, such as buildings and equipment? If so, why are they viewed differently? Explain.

2. Should the development of data to prove that pirates actually create the "buzz" that promotes profits for rights holders have any bearing at all on discussions of how to deal with compliance and its cost?

3. Should the federal government require state governments and private institutions to take on the cost of this responsibility merely because their "customers" are possibly members of the population of pirates? Could the same argument be applied to the rights holders represented by the RIAA, whose "customers" are also members of this population?

4. If higher ed closed the accounts of student violators, could the problem of illegal file sharing be solved? Is it pragmatic for students to purchase their own online accounts, especially when the accounts are generally free of charge from services such as Gmail and Yahoo? Are there other concerns that would inevitably follow?

5. Could schools disrupt service to these accounts on campus in order to lessen the cost of enforcement? Would there be other technical advantages to this alternative? What would be the disadvantage? What is the policy at other institutions of higher learning and at secondary institutions?

Key Terms

1. Graduated response system

2. HEOA

FORUM 6
Human Evolution and Technology

Ask anyone who was assigned to read the novel *1984* near the time of that actual year, and you may find a reaction similar to mine. I was at Notre Dame Academy for Girls in Miami, Florida, where the majority of my classmates' families had fled their homelands for political asylum within the previous two decades. Those first-generation Americans often made references to the privileges of living in a democracy, and our responsibilities as citizens to protect them. I can still envision the passion of my influential Cuban-born English teacher, Mrs. Rivera. With a Suze-Orman-like rapid-fire, finger movement, directed not at us, but at her brain, she gave concrete clarity to a priceless intangible asset, "They can take away everything you own, your life savings, your home, even your family…but they can never, never take away this." She implored us to understand the everlasting value of our cognitive properties. Exclusively ours and ours alone, it encompasses our ability to attain knowledge and information, and to use it to think critically. Yet even with this foundation, in our classroom discussions of an Orwellian society, we vigorously denied the prospect that Americans would ever accept the use of technology to routinely monitor the movements and conversations of its citizens, let alone track our thinking through our digital breadcrumbs to be sold to marketers as a commodity. Moreover, with our fingers still caught between the keys of obsolete manual typewriters, we viewed this surveillance technology as mere science fiction.

In light of the exponential progression of technological advances in recent years, researchers suggest that we consider the impact of the use of technology on the human condition in the longer term. Dr. Glenn Wilson, at the University of London, found the constant distraction of "always on" technology, or "infomania," to temporarily decrease intelligence quotient (IQ) by as much as 10 points (Horsnell, 2005). Dr. Oliver Curry of the London School of Economics suggests that the impact of technology on human evolution is possible (Firth, 2007). He theorizes that our dependence on technology and medical intervention may cause our decline. Although he expects progress over the next millennium, he believes humans will peak in the year 3000, and then begin to decline. He predicts that in about the year 12000, there will be a notable decrease in communication skills and emotions, such as love, sympathy, and trust, and no concept of team play. Curry further projects that in 100,000 years, technology dependence may cause a possible split into two different species, genetic haves and have-nots; one that is intelligent and creative, and one that is dim-witted. While the latter may ring as fantasy, I am once again compelled to ponder the naiveté of my past. I recall another science fiction novel I read in high school, *The Time Machine* by H. G. Wells, which stands as a classic glimpse 800,000 years into the future—a must read!

Article: Will we one day find technology on our family tree?

By J. Scott Orr
April 17, 2008
Newhouse News Service

There is no doubt recent years have brought advances in technology that have been revolutionary, but are they also evolutionary?

Whether technology will have an impact on the evolution of the human species is a controversial question, but there already are signs that we are using our brains differently today than people did just a generation ago.

Quick, how many telephone numbers have you committed to memory? Probably not as many as you did before you started storing contacts in your cell phone. Do you use your brain, or a calculator, to answer math problems? Why memorize facts when all the world's information is as close as the nearest Internet connection?

Today's technological advances are, of course, a mere blip on the human evolutionary timeline, but there are certainly precedents for technology playing a role in previous episodes of human evolution, like breakthroughs in the creation and use of hunting tools or the development of agriculture tens of thousands of years ago. William Halal, a professor of science, technology and innovation at George Washington University and author of the forthcoming book "Technology's Promise," said he sees the coming decades as a time of major change for technology and the human condition.

By 2020, Halal predicts, artificial intelligence, robotics and other technologies will advance to the point where they take over many of the mundane tasks humans now perform both physically and mentally. That, he said, is good because it will free up the world's human resources to deal with more pressing global concerns.

"All of the routine things we currently preoccupy ourselves with are going to disappear and people are going to do what? We will move up another notch in the level of evolution," he said.

"Humans are going to move on to higher-order functions that are going to be needed to address these enormous challenges that will face the world," he said, citing global issues such as international conflict, energy depletion, climate change, environmental degradation and weapons of mass destruction.

"This will be a very promising period in the history of man," Halal said.

Patrick Tucker, director of communications for the World Future Society and senior editor of the Futurist magazine, said new technologies that enable humans to avoid mundane mental and physical tasks could lead to generations of people who are less physically able.

There already is evidence humans are doing less physically. Not long ago, for example, if you were seeking the answer to a complicated question you had to go to the library, or grab a book from a shelf, physically open it and look for the answer. Now, you just type your query into an Internet search engine like Google. Soon, you'll ask your computer the question verbally, eliminating even the use of your fingers to access information.

"We are the first humans to outsource jobs to technology, to automate that which is labor intensive or mentally tedious," said Tucker. "In the 21st century, this may result in people that are by and large less capable than we are today. Whether or not we seize all of those opportunities depends on how we mature in the coming decades."

So if today's humans are devoting fewer resources to things like rote memorization of phone numbers or mathematical calculations, where is all that brain power going? Maybe it's going to develop more technology, says Peter Rojas, writer and creator of a tech review site, who is devoting his energies to music publishing as CEO of rcrdlbl.com. "I think it is a big advantage that people who have grown up in the digital era have an innate sense of what information is worth internalizing and what is not," Rojas said. "Not that it is not valuable to know things, but being able to access and discover and find information is in some ways more important."

"There are a lot of other important things we use our brains for that aren't memorization, like learning to think abstractly and creatively to develop new stuff," he said.

But those who look at things in an evolutionary context say modern technological changes are not likely to affect significantly the human species because while technology might change human behavior—the way we think or other aspects of our humanity—it also can supply solutions that prevent our genes from dealing with our problems.

John Hawks, a professor of anthropology at the University of Wisconsin, explained evolution is all about natural selection and genes, and humans have evolved because superior genes led to the procreation and survival of those with the most robust genetic makeup.

Today, things like diminished eyesight because of overexposure to computer screens for example, can easily be corrected with glasses or surgery and therefore won't affect the human gene pool.

"Sitting in front of a computer all day, you are using your eyes differently than if you're hunting all day in the wild, but there is not a genetic susceptibility there. Our population is not going to evolve because of these things," Hawks said.

"There are all kinds of technologies to deal with things like diseases, obesity, addiction. There are technologies that are there to address changes in humans that may be brought on by the use of technology. Our genes in some sense don't have to respond."

Still, Stanley Ambrose, a professor of anthropology at the University of Illinois, at least allows for the possibility that technology could be having an impact on human evolution. But like all evolutionary ideas, the question will not be answered over mere generations, but over thousands of years.

Take for example the human thumb, which throughout history has been used in opposition to fingers for grasping things. Today, the thumb has taken on new prominence among digits as it is used more and more to operate handheld communication devices.

"There may be some genetically based extra neural connection that could allow me to text message faster," Ambrose said. "Faster text messaging could get me a better job and allow me to have more kids to inherit my thumb gene. That would be evolving."

He added, however, if there were a text-messaging gene, it might already have been present in humans, but stayed dormant until a use for it came about.

"People could have been evolving a better text-messaging thumb gene for 100,000 years, but it didn't do any good until BlackBerrys came around. It could be a capacity that some had that suddenly became advantageous," Ambrose said.

Taking Halal's theory of more brains, less physicality to its extreme, is it possible too many advances in technology could lead to a race of transhumans, morphed into physically challenged brainiacs? Could the human race one day become mere brains, like "The Providers" featured in an early "Star Trek" episode, or more like super-smart, but physically able beings like Mr. Spock?

These are choices tomorrow's humans will have to make for themselves, says Tucker of the World Future Society.

"No one, I think, would make the decision, looking forward to future technologies, where I am nothing more than a brain in a jar, capable of unimaginable feats of intellectual dexterity but bound to float in the ether for eternity," he said.

Things to Think About

1. What is infomania and how does it impact an organization? Managers at Intel and U.S. Cellular are declaring "Zero E-mail Fridays." Could this be a reaction to the lost productivity of infomania? Explain how Zero E-mail Fridays could improve productivity.

2. If IQ were truly found to be temporarily lost, why are researchers concerned about a permanent impact on human evolution? Can the repetitive nature of producing the lower quotient cause a permanent effect?

3. What impact could the use of technology have on human creativity? While some point out negative effects, could technology also impact creativity in a positive manner? Explain.

4. Will robotics replace creativity in the performing arts? If it is possible that a robot violinist could replace a human one in the New York Philharmonic, could the interest of young talented musicians diminish as a result?

5. An editorial was written in the *Washington Post* in which a physician expressed concern that children use the computer to communicate so often that they have difficulty writing both in print and cursive. He suggested that technology should be kept out of the hands of young children. Provide arguments for both sides of this issue.

Key Terms

1. Infomania

2. Hygiene hypothesis

FORUM 7
Internet Censorship

S hould industry be held accountable as an accomplice in the violation of human rights? The technology industry claims that U.S. trade agreements have not done enough to ensure freedom of information over the Internet. And human rights groups have called for a regulatory framework from Congress with penalties for industry violators. Can the three sometimes opposing viewpoints work together to agree upon mutually acceptable terms?

Public concern has grown over the past two years in response to such incidents as Yahoo's admission to providing information that identified two journalists who were later arrested and imprisoned.

One response has been the Global Network Initiative (http://www.globalnetworkinitiative.org), whose participants include Google, Microsoft, Yahoo, and, at present, 21 other organizations. Their mission is "to enable companies and their stakeholders to assist those in the Information and Communication technology industry to respect and protect freedom of expression and privacy globally through individual and collective actions." Each organization has agreed to specific principles, implementation guidelines and governance, and an accountability and learning framework that appears rigorous and challenging.

A perusal of this site may prove hopeful to the strongest of skeptics.

Article: Cisco Systems denies online censorship role in China

By Dibya Sarkar
May 20, 2008
USA Today

WASHINGTON—A Cisco Systems executive told a Senate subcommittee Tuesday that comments in an internal document about China's goal to "combat" a religious group did not reflect the company's views on censorship.

The PowerPoint presentation, which described China's technology status, included a slide that referred to goals to stop network-related crimes, guarantee the security and services of a public network and "combat 'Falun Gong' evil religion and other hostiles." Falun Gong is a spiritual movement banned by the Chinese government, which considers it a dangerous cult.

"In no case does the document propose that any Cisco products be provided to facilitate the political goals of the government and no reference to applications of our products to the goals of censorship or monitoring," Cisco general counsel Mark Chandler told the Senate Judiciary subcommittee on human rights and the law.

The subcommittee heard testimony from Cisco, Google, and Yahoo executives about how U.S. Internet and technology companies do business with certain governments that censor and suppress the free speech of their citizens.

Chandler said that Cisco regrets that comments from a Chinese government official were included in the 2002 presentation, which also mentioned other technology projects.

However, Shiyu Zhou, deputy director of the humans rights group Global Internet Freedom Consortium, said Cisco's presentation offered planning, construction, technical training and other services to help China improve law enforcement and security network operations.

"Cisco can no longer assure Congress that Cisco China had not been and is not now an accomplice in partnering with China's Internet repression," he said during the hearing. "And, whether directly or indirectly, in the persecution of Falun Gong practitioners and other peaceful citizens in China."

U.S. companies have come under an enormous amount of scrutiny and criticism as they do business in countries, such as China, that actively limit citizen access to information on the Web or who have used personally identifiable information to track down dissidents.

"This is not a black and white issue. This is not an easy issue," said Sen. Richard Durbin, D-Ill., the subcommittee's chair.

Since the start of 2007, Google services—including its YouTube video sharing, blogging and social networking sites—have been blocked in whole or in part in 27 countries, such as China, Turkey and Myanmar, said Nicole Wong, Google's deputy general counsel.

While American tech companies face challenges in dealing with repressive governments, Durbin said those difficulties doesn't excuse those that have fallen short of their moral obligation, which could be made into a legal obligation.

Rep. Chris Smith, R-N.J., last year introduced a House bill that would bar U.S. Internet companies from turning over personally identifiable information to governments that use it to suppress dissent. If the tech companies gave up information, they could face criminal penalties. Durbin said the Senate may consider similar legislation.

Yahoo has been a target of U.S. lawmakers and human rights groups for the last two years after admitting it provided information to Chinese authorities that led to the arrests and imprisonment of two Chinese journalists.

Since then, the Sunnyvale, Calif.-based company has settled a lawsuit with the journalists' families and established a human rights fund to provide humanitarian and legal aid to dissidents.

Both Google and Yahoo said the U.S. government and other countries need to make Internet freedom a top priority.

"We have asked the U.S. government to use its leverage—through trade relationships, bilateral and multilateral forums, and other diplomatic means—to create a global environment where Internet freedom is a priority and where people are no longer imprisoned for expressing their views online," said Michael Samway, Yahoo's vice president and general counsel.

However, Arvind Ganesan, a program director at Human Rights Watch, said companies, including Google, aren't taking their ethical principles seriously.

Over the last 18 months, industry, academics and human rights groups have been working on a voluntary code of conduct for companies doing business in repressive countries. The code, when finished, would include an enforcement process and independent monitoring, an element some companies are fighting.

Although a voluntary approach is a good start, Ganesan said, it likely won't go far enough. Human Rights Watch endorses a regulatory framework, including penalties to hold companies accountable.

Things to Think About

1. What if foreign government use of information was not known prior to providing the information? Would this be enforceable under the proposed law from Rep. Chris Smith's introduced bill?

2. As of January 26, 2009, it is illegal in Britain to possess pornographic pictures that the government deems to be extreme. Is this censorship or common sense protection?

3. Privacy International and the Greennet Educational Trust have funded research in corporate censorship. "*Some American cable companies seek to turn the Internet into a controlled distribution medium like TV and radio, and are putting in changes to the Internet's infrastructure…Protection of corporate intellectual property has resulted in…deterioration in trust across the Internet.*" Do we expect the Internet to emulate the role of other media outlets?

4. When Cisco is hosted by a government that does not share the same views on Internet censorship as the United States, to whom does the company owe its primary allegiance?

5. Is there such a thing as justified and appropriate censorship? Explain. Do you think a voluntary approach to a regulatory censorship framework will work?

Key Terms

1. Internet censorship

2. Accountability

FORUM 8
Usability: Electronic Voting Systems

Chad was a very popular name for boys born around 1970. In fact, I once had a colleague named Chad who was named after his father, Charles. And although the name's popularity appeared to gradually lessen until about 1999, according to the chart at http://www.thinkbabynames.com, it took a more precipitous decline after the year 2000. It was that year that informed citizens around the globe learned the real meaning of the word.

A chad is a piece of paper. Specifically, it is a very small fragment of paper. In large quantities, it works well as confetti. When you use a hole punch to punch a hole in paper, a chad falls to the ground.

In the year 2000, Florida voters expected to create chads as a byproduct of using a Votomatic punch card ballot to vote. But there was a problem. Many of the voting machines had never been cleaned of the chads that remained from numerous previous elections. So when voters arrived at the polls in 2000 in Florida, there was little or no space in the area behind the ballot card—not enough for a new chad. Imagine an attempt to punch a hole in paper if there was a wall behind the paper. You would not create a hole at all and would not produce a chad. If there was just a tiny bit of space, you, like the voters, might create a hanging chad (a chad attached to the ballot card at one corner), or a swinging chad (a chad attached at two corners), a tri chad (a chad attached to three corners), a dimpled chad (an indentation indicating where the voter may have intended to mark the ballot), or a pregnant chad (most often considered a greater mark than a dimpled chad). The bottom line is that it was reported that thousands of votes were never counted, a condition called "under votes." In a democracy, a government by the people and for the people, the right to vote is at the core of its existence; many of our ancestors gave their lives to defend the right to vote. Imagine learning that your vote did not count because the system had not been maintained! (http://americanhistory.si.edu/VOTE/florida.html)

In technical terms, the usability and ballot design factors were responsible for problems such as these. In the system development life cycle (SDLC), we know that it is imperative that systems be tested before implementation, and maintained after that, addressing the inevitable new problems, creating new designs, testing , implementing, maintaining, and on and on and the cycle (a Greek word for "circle") continues. If the cycle is broken, in time, the system usually fails.

Of course, we might have recognized the failure of this system at a later time except that the U.S. presidential election of 2000 was the closest since 1876. Students too young to remember the commotion created by the election of 2000 are stunned to recognize that at the height of the Information Age it took almost five weeks and a Supreme Court decision to name our new president (Raskin, 2003).

As with most problems, we tend to find a silver lining. In this case, this event spurred the installation of electronic voting machines in Florida and around the country. The Help America Vote Act (HAVA) was passed to help states upgrade their election technology (http://www.fec.gov/hava/hava.htm). But were our problems solved?

Article: Stumper's Handy Voting-Problem Primer

By Sarah Kliff
October 21, 2008
Newsweek

Voting machines in Beaufort County, South Carolina weren't working when early voting started on Oct. 6. The problem? The state had given local election officials the wrong password to format the machines. Machines in Jacksonville, Fla. wouldn't record ballots. In Houston, ID scanning machines broke down, leaving about 300 voters waiting in line. "I came out here just expecting to shake people's hands and it's pandemonium," Representative Shelia Jackson Lee told the Houston Chronicle.

Early voting kicks off and, no surprise, a slew of mini-meltdowns follows. This is just the beginning of it: experts readily admit that somewhere, in some unforeseen county, there will be a voting breakdown—machines that don't record votes or tallies that don't add up. As election day nears, the more difficult question is: Will it be similar to 2000 in Florida—a recount fiasco that stretches on for weeks—or 2004 in Ohio, where problems with provisional ballots were resolved relatively quickly? And which unforeseen county will become the electoral scapegoat? Achieving that level of specificity is a bit harder.

"There will be some close election, even if it's not presidential, where they don't have proper procedures in place and things break down," says Larry Norden, project director at New York University's Brennan Center for Justice. Norden's new, 190-page report asks, "Is America Ready to Vote?" The answer: sort of. He and his co-authors found nine states largely unprepared for the election, including key swing states like Colorado and Virginia. Ironically, the majority of the most prepared states—California, Oregon, Alaska, Wisconsin—aren't really in play (Missouri is one exception). **Sarah Kliff** touched base with Norden about the potential problem spots and what voters can do about them. His take on what we're in for this time around:

Ohio and Florida still have meltdown potential, but not for the same reasons as before. They're among the growing number of states that require an exact match between a voter's ID and his or her voter registration information. These "no-match, no-vote" policies mean that any typo or nickname can get you disqualified. Norden uses himself as an example: he's Larry on his driver's license, Lawrence on his voter registration and, if he's in a "no match, no vote" state," he won't be voting. Both Ohio and Florida—two of the top swing states—have these policies. In Ohio, things look particularly grim: about 200,000 of the 660,000 voters who have registered there since Jan. 1 have records that don't match other government databases—and, on Friday, the Supreme Court ruled that Ohio's top election officials do not have to do more to help counties verify voter eligibility. Those 200,000 disputed registrations are a serious concern in a swing state where the Republican margin of victory was only 119,000 votes last time around.

Change: not just a campaign slogan. Two-thirds of voters will use a voting technology that's different from the one they used in the last presidential election, raising the risk of human error. The changes may vex election workers as well. If a county switches from electronic voting machines to paper ballots, for example—as many did this time around—officials need to create and follow an entirely new set of procedures. This is one of the problems that has plagued Palm Beach, where new technology played a major role in their latest voting meltdown.

High Turnout + Mechanical Failures = Recipe for Disaster. Record turnout and overwhelmed polling stations are basically a given after the massive crowds that turned out for the primaries. What could really cause a meltdown is if voting machines begin to malfunction and polling stations don't have a back-up plan. It's not an unlikely situation: by Norden's count, the majority of states do not have a policy to deal with voting machines gone haywire. This could be particularly problematic in some key swing states. Pennsylvania, for example, does not mandate that polling stations switch to emergency paper ballots unless all voting machines are down. So if half the machines go down, Norden says, lines could become four or five hours long. Without an emergency option, voters would likely get discouraged and go home. In Virginia, there's no statewide policy on how to deal with a mechanical malfunction, which will probably be a bigger problem for voters using electronic ballots. "Places that use paper usually have some indication that they're running low," says Norden. "Whereas if a machine breaks down, you didn't have any warning, and then you're stuck."

Voters can't fix everything—but they can fix some things. Here comes the public service announcement—what you, dear reader, can do to make this election a smooth one. First, make sure you're registered. It seems obvious, Norden says, but between 2004 and 2006, the states collectively purged 13 million voters. Purges are meant to remove the deceased and departed from the rolls, but they're prone to error and partisan manipulation (in Mississippi, for example, one election official purged 10,000 voters a week before the primary—from her home computer). While you're at it, double check your polling location, too. "In many states, if you vote at the wrong location, it won't count," Norden explains. A good place to find the necessary information, he says, is www.govote.org. And don't forget to check out a sample ballot—especially if you're among those two-thirds of Americans who will be grappling with a new technology on Election Day.

Last but not least, do your Democratic duty. "Barring some major breakdown in the system, which occasionally happens, the vast, vast majority of votes will count," says Norden. "So you should get out and vote." In the meantime, pray that we don't end up with Florida: The Sequel.

Things to Think About

1. What can the election workers do to minimize problem areas on Election Day?

2. Is voter turnout related to the effectiveness of electronic voting? Explain.

3. Is the old-fashioned paper ballot more reliable than technology? Would the system benefit from parallel implementation?

4. What can the voting public do to minimize voting problems? How can government assist them? How can government assist states in order to avoid the meltdown potential?

5. Explain how to use the SDLC for today's systems. Investigate the problems that occurred during the last federal election.

Key Terms

1. Meltdown potential

2. Electoral scapegoat

FORUM 9
Open Source Software

During my recent stay at the Marriott Hotel, I opted to use the lobby computer. To my surprise, I found OpenOffice.org instead of Microsoft Office. I have used the cross-platform open source suite software in the past and have required my students to gain familiarity with all four programs, Writer, Calc, Base, and Impress, since these programs are compatible with Word, Excel, Access, and PowerPoint. Users can edit and save a file in OpenOffice.org that was created in Microsoft Office and vice versa. Although the electronic spreadsheet, Calc, does not compare to the powerful provisions offered by Excel, for the use of many functions, Calc is sufficient. Never again should a college professor hear that a student cannot afford to purchase necessary productivity software. Open source, however, is even available for more technical software uses, such as the need for collections of useful tools installed on a bootable CD that can be used during a computer forensics investigation. Helix, for example, is freely downloadable at http://www.e-fense.com/helix (Austin, 2007).

The 60s represented the advent of English type higher level programs such as COBOL (Common Business Oriented Language) and BASIC (Dartmouth, 1964); the 70s represented the development and acceptance of the microcomputer; the 80s gave us preprogrammed application software; and the 90s brought us software suites and the commercialization of the Internet. The decade between 2000 and 2010 is often referred to as the "oughties," which the Urban Dictionary explains as having evolved from the word "ought," a British word for "zero," which represents zero cost (Urban, 2009). Students of the oughties use open source and freeware programs, which appear to have revolutionized the university environment as well as small businesses for research and communication. Examples of this free software abound.

Linux is a powerful operating system. BitTorrent is a program that will allow you to download large files such as video files (only legal ones, please). Skype is easy to use as a Voice over Internet Protocol, not only to meet with your project team through voice, but for video conferencing. Twitter is a powerful microblogging tool that will keep your team informed of every new development instantly. Diigo is a bookmarking tool, also enabling highlighting and electronic sticky notes and the use of their hardware for saving your research; it interfaces well with Google Reader, a Web-based aggregator that will do much of your research for you. With Google Trends, you can export a csv (comma separated value) file that indicates data that uses Google search entries as the basis for indication of interest trends in the marketplace. With Google Apps and Dropbox, you can edit a report and save it within a "cloud" (remote server) on the Internet for your team members to review and edit, saving a new document while maintaining the original one, without the need to maintain the hardware and software of the infrastructure that stores your work.

For example, simply go to your favorite newspaper Web sites, such as the *Asbury Park Press*, *TechRepublic*, *Wired*, the *Wall Street Journal*, and the *New York Times*, and scroll down to select the RSS (Really Simple Syndication) feed button. You'll now receive constantly updated headlines both online and offline within the Google Reader interface. Using Diigo, bookmark the article, attach notes, and tag Web pages. Remember, Diigo is just as handy for conducting literary research using electronic library resources, such as ProQuest. As these are collaborative Web 2.0 tools, you will have the choice to make your notes public or private and can create an alias account for sharing with your research team members. As you and your team members seek to make changes to your shared report, you will invite them to the report using Google Apps. Instead of sending an attachment to each of your team members, you will send your teammates to the attachment.

Browsers you may be unfamiliar with include a three dimensional one found at *http://spacetime.com* and Opera, a browser that appears to move quicker than others as it transfers Web pages.

Even extranet systems in education, often known as "eCampus," can now switch to an open source alternative. Moodle is free of charge and installed at numerous institutions. When adopting Moodle, some institutions outsource the management of Moodle to third party service providers who specialize in customizing and managing it, for a fraction of the cost of using other packages from vendors such as Blackboard, WebCT, or Desire 2 Learn. Library Management Systems are also available in open source. They include programs such as Koha, Evergreen, and OPALS (Open-source-Automated Library Management System). Hosting firms, such as Equinox Software, are often contracted to implement and maintain the open source system at a fraction of the cost of using proprietary software (Devaney, 2009).

Microsoft recently announced the end of Encarta, the electronic encyclopedia that could not compete with the free use of Wikipedia (Crovitz, 2009). If you use Wikipedia for research, go to *http://Vispedia.stanford.edu* to pick up a button to place on your toolbar to provide a visual interactive interface for Wikipedia. Data is selected from a Wikipedia table after it has been verified from the sources provided by Wikipedia at the bottom of the page, or from other sources. You select the field names for the query table, and the data is then automatically entered on a map, timeline, scatter plot, or circular tree plot in color. The file may be saved as a csv (comma separated value) file, used for data in table form, and exported, or it can be embedded as Flash code or an image file.

Other open source applications include the use of Process Explorer to detect malware. As a system optimization tool to remove files no longer needed, such as that which may be found in the registry, as well as temporary Internet files and cookies, CCleaner is available. Finally, if users are interested in starting a blog, an open source program called WordPress hosts 12 million blogs and features reader stats and page-flip photos galleries. It is used by *CNN*, *The New York Times*, *Coca-Cola*, and many other industry giants.

Another added benefit to switching to open source may be an improvement in speed on your computer. Switched.com, for example, suggests that moving to the use of different applications is one of the most overlooked ways to speed up your PC. Switch endorses VLC Media Player to replace Windows Media Player and Foxit to replace Adobe Reader (O'Brien, 2009).

In a time of economic downturn, it has never been simpler to find powerful open source tools for free.

Article: Treat Yourself to a Suite Alternative: OpenOffice.org 3.0

By Jason Brooks
October 12, 2008
San Francisco Technology Examiner

OpenOffice.org 3.0 is a great suite of office productivity applications (word processor, spreadsheet, presentation & database) that's very similar to Microsoft Office in function, and very different in price. Where pricing for Microsoft Office 2007 starts around $100, you can download and use OpenOffice.org 3.0 for free.

In fact, since OpenOffice.org 3.0 is open source software, it's also free to redistribute. In other words, if somebody asks you for a copy of your office suite, you can hand it over without worrying that some coalition of willing FBI & Interpol agents might swing through your windows, National Lampoon's Christmas Vacation style, to redress your copyright abuses.

Next to its free-ness, the best thing about OpenOffice.org is that it will run quite happily on your computer, whether you're a PC, a Mac, or a nerdy user of Linux or Solaris.

Mac users who have taken OpenOffice.org for a spin in the past will appreciate the way that version 3.0 blends naturally into OS X's Aqua interface—previous versions of the suite for the Mac required the X11 subsystem from Apple to run, and these versions didn't seem very Mac-like in their operation.

PowerPC Mac-heads take note, however, this Aquafied version is for Intel Macs only—check out http://www.neooffice.org for a PPC-friendly option.

Now that we've established that OpenOffice.org will run on your computer—pretty much no matter what—you may be wondering whether this free suite will work with your Microsoft Office files.

OpenOffice.org will indeed open files created in Microsoft Office, and you can modify these files and save them back to Office format, as well as create new Office-formatted files. By default, OpenOffice.org does not save file in Microsoft formats, although you can change this, if you wish.

The reason for this file format proliferation is that until very recently, Microsoft kept the details of its document formats secret. Rather than depend on an incomplete understanding of a reverse-engineered document format, the creators of OpenOffice.org joined a group of other projects and companies to spec out a new, standardized format: the OpenDocument Format.

Today, OpenOffice.org uses ODF, as does IBM's Lotus Symphony, Google's Docs and Spreadsheets, Zoho Office, and others. Even Microsoft, which initially declined to join the ODF group, has announced its plans to add ODF support to Office 2007 early next year.

OpenOffice.org does a very good job with the file formats from Microsoft's pre-2007 Office releases (.doc, .xls, .ppt) and does a pretty good job with the new Office 2007 formats (.docx, .xlsx, .pptx).

My generic advice around office application file formats is that if you want to make sure that a document arrives at its destination looking exactly the way you intended, you should save it in Adobe's PDF format. Helpfully, OpenOffice.org includes a PDF export feature.

So OpenOffice.org works with the Microsoft files you might receive, and it provides a bulletproof means of controlling the way your documents look when you send them to other people. Perhaps the next logical question is whether OpenOffice.org does everything that Microsoft Office does.

It's safe to say that OpenOffice.org does not do everything that Microsoft Office does. I mean, does anyone, either within Microsoft or without, really even know everything that Office can do? How many clicks would it take to spelunk Office's depths These are koan-like questions, and each of the past three Microsoft Office releases has been designed primarily around the riddle of exposing more of these features to Office users; Microsoft calls this quest Discoverability.

I've been using OpenOffice.org for about six years now, and I can report the suite performs all of the Office features that I either know about, or was accustomed to using in Office. OpenOffice.org doesn't always handle things as elegantly as Office does, but it gets the job done.

For instance, a couple of releases ago, Microsoft added a nifty feature in Word in which pasting text from the Web into a document would spawn a little unobtrusive dialog offering to strip out the formatting of what you just pasted. I can't stand formatting junk buildup in my documents, so I thought this was a super feature.

In OpenOffice.org, there's no magically appearing mini dialog, but I can hit ctrl-shift-V to "Paste Special," (as opposed to the regular ctrl-V for regular paste) to have the option of pasting as plain text. A less-fancy implementation, but 100% functionally equivalent.

My needs are fairly modest: I write, edit, and pass around documents in the OpenOffice.org word processor, I crunch fantasy basketball stats in its spreadsheet application, and I use the presentation application to open up the PowerPoint slide decks I receive, convert them to PDFs, and follow along on conference calls in a simple PDF viewer.

I am, however, looking forward to expanding that fantasy stat analysis for the 2008 season using OpenOffice.org 3.0's shiny new Solver feature for working out multi-variable scenarios.

Your mileage will definitely vary, and how much it varies depends on just how you use these productivity applications. Although, given the fact that OpenOffice.org is one free 150MB-ish download away, it can't hurt to give it a run in your own productivity environment.

Weigh in with your reactions in the space below. I'd love to hear how you fare.

Things to Think About

1. Describe open source software. Why do programmers unite to produce it?

2. After using OpenOffice 3.0, list the advantages and disadvantages of the software over Microsoft Office 2007.

3. What is "discoverability" with regard to software? Explain.

4. How would you describe the "usability" of OpenOffice 3.0? Should cost be an important consideration in weighing the decision to adopt the software?

5. How much of a concern is security when using open source software? Describe the concerns and realities, and actions suggested to minimize the risks.

Key Terms

1. Open source software

2. RSS feed

FORUM 10
Microblogging and Office Productivity

Twitter Nation is a large community of rapid growth in which text messages are sent to multiple individuals within a public or private community. Twitter is attributed to the success of the political campaign of President Obama, as interested citizens were able to follow Obama's every step on the campaign trail. No matter what the political affiliation of the observer, it was considered a brilliant strategy to promote a special connection among those who chose to be members of his community.

The act of microblogging "tweets" has been found to be particularly productive for the short snippets of communication required by some professions. Other early adopters have included emergency responders, several members of Congress, fire fighters, and CNN anchorpersons, who used it both in the field and on air in the newsroom. Two recent and highly publicized airplane accidents, one in Denver and the other in the Hudson River, New York, had passengers who used Twitter for contact, reinforcing its value to the public in relation to its response to emergencies. Finally, Twitter is growing by leaps and bounds as an answer to project team members in business in order to keep colleagues at work "in-the-know" immediately, in a manner that may be no longer manageable by email.

But for all its success, like any electronic mode of communication, the user needs to be thoughtful about how, when, and where it is used. Recently, a U.S. Senator sent a tweet to his constituents while in Iraq. He received considerable criticism amidst accusations of having jeopardized the safety of those accompanying him on his travel (Oliphant, 2009).

In addition, as it is used on an electronic device, it is open to security exploits. Recently, just after a music awards presentation, a "clickjacking" virus interrupted those in attendance. Another recent security exploit involved erroneous tweets emanating from the hacking of the celebrity accounts of Britney Spears, Bill O'Reilly, and President Obama's account, used before his inauguration (Arrington, 2009).

Having recently received $35 million from venture investors, Twitter appears to be an active member of cyberspace for some time to come.

Article: Will Microblogging at Work Make You More Productive?

By Claire Cain Miller
October 21, 2008
The New York Times

On Tuesday, The Times published an article I wrote about Twitter and Yammer, two microblogging services that let users blast short messages to a group of virtual followers. Twitter has gotten a lot of buzz since it was created in 2006. Yammer is new on the scene, just six weeks old, with a different goal: to be Twitter for businesses.

Yammer was created for employees of Geni, a family tree Web site. When they discovered how useful it was for them, David Sacks, the founder of Geni, decided to spin Yammer off into its own company with $1 million of Geni's venture funding. Mr. Sacks, a PayPal co-founder, now runs both start-ups and is raising a new round of funding for Yammer.

On Twitter, people write about the important and the mundane, like, "At school and debating whether I should have more coffee." With a workplace focus, Yammer will not deal in such trivialities, Mr. Sacks said. "People don't want to hear from their friends five times a day about what they're doing. But they do want to hear from their co-workers five times a day about what they're working on," he said.

The central question on Twitter, "What are you doing?" is transformed on Yammer to, "What are you working on?" There are other features specific to the office. Unlike Twitter, which limits users to 140 characters, Yammer's users can type as much as they want and reply to specific messages. They can attach photos, documents or videos. Yammer also has user profiles and will soon add groups, so people can have conversations that other employees cannot see. It has plans to include vendors or consultants outside the company network. Users can check Yammer and post updates from the Web, instant message services or phones.

And just why do we need this when e-mail and instant messaging do similar things?

E-mail no longer serves its proper purpose, which is to request an active response, Mr. Sacks said. All the rest of the stuff that clogs in-boxes—mass e-mails sharing a link to an article, for example, or notifications of company events—makes e-mail less efficient. He wants to move all that to Yammer.

Mr. Sacks believes that Yammer can rise above all that. "If we're successful, ultimately people will see e-mail and I.M. as simply delivery channels for Yammer content," he said.

On a recent day at Yammer, for example, one employee sent around a link to an article about a new social networking experiment at Yahoo. The company's lawyer wrote that he was working on employee stock option agreements and several employees responded with questions about the options package. Someone announced that the catered lunch menu included California rolls and chicken kebabs.

Yammer is free for anyone with a company e-mail address. Mr. Sacks hopes that it spreads within companies and catches the eye of the higher-ups. At that point, a worried I.T. employee or executive usually calls Yammer and asks about the security features. Those include limiting the I.P. addresses that can read a company account, requiring passwords, cutting off ex-employees and removing certain messages. Once a company administrator takes over, Yammer charges $1 per user per month.

Mr. Sacks hopes to skirt the I.T. department and empower employees. "Instead of the most jaded person about new technology in the company making the decision, the most forward-thinking person in the company can do it," he said. People are itching to use the Web tools they use at home in the office, he said, and this is a way to speed the process. It also saves Yammer money on an expensive enterprise salesforce.

Some people have complained that this strategy is tantamount to blackmail, Mr. Sacks said, because it forces companies to sign up to control it since their employees are already using it. He disagrees—an I.T. department can always block Yammer's Web site, he pointed out.

In the first six weeks, 60,000 users have signed on, and 4,000 of them have convinced their companies to pay. People at Cisco Systems, Xerox and Hewlett-Packard use it. Mr. Sacks has received calls from a farm equipment supplier with thousands of remote sales reps, a motion picture company that already has 400 employees using Yammer and a casino company that has 25,000 employees in other countries.

Yammer is a new way to do a lot of stuff we already do at work. Social enterprise software like Clearspace from Jive Software and SharePoint from Microsoft offer some of these features. Companies already use Twitter and Facebook to communicate with co-workers. For many years, instant messaging has been solving a lot of the problems that Mr. Sacks has with e-mail.

What do you think? Do workers need a new way to communicate? Or will Yammer be yet another inbox to keep up with in an already cluttered digital world?

Things to Think About

1. List the ways workers communicate with each other. Categorize the determination to use each particular medium by its purpose. Does Yammer give workers something that was previously missing? Explain.

2. Explain how workers might abuse Yammer if it is not controlled by the organization.

3. Should there be a concern that workers' productivity might decrease in relation to the time they utilize software on the Web? Does the advent of Web 2.0 and cloud computing make that concern moot? Explain.

4. Would it be necessary to adopt guidelines for microblogging etiquette if it were to be adopted? What suggestions would you make in that regard?

5. With the adoption of microblogging, VoIP, and "everything digital," rather than analog, could all communication in relation to a particular topic or client be saved in the same file instantly, within a communication system such as Outlook? What software is available currently?

Key Terms

1. VoIP

2. Yammer

FORUM 11
Online Personal Health Records and Privacy

"Security is now down to the document level," explained Mary Beth Haugen, Director of Information Management Services in Denver, a statement that could be said to sum up the greatest challenge to patient privacy (Wagley, 2008). In January 2009, in the midst of a global economic crisis, world citizens watched as the U.S. Congress passed a $787 billion economic stimulus bill that will pour over $20 billion into the U.S. health care system in order to build an electronic infrastructure to hold your personal data (phprivacy.net, 2009). Just how secure is your data? Recent research reveals that the greatest vulnerability is not from external hackers, but from those within. Health organizations are full of opportunities that create a fertile ground for exploitation. Employees of all levels of education and job status—part-time, temporary, and volunteer, and most hired with limited or no background investigation—work in a system that historically has permitted their access to private patient records. Two high profile cases serve to highlight the culture. Twenty-seven health care workers were suspended for peering at George Clooney's records. Another hospital worker, found later to have already been reprimanded once for violating patient privacy rights, was fired for sharing Britney Spears' records (Wagley, 2008).

As we move toward a greater level of access to information, the health care industry has agreed to adopt new privacy policies that are widely used in information assurance and surveillance in government. For example, just as FBI source data may be relegated to various classifications of security, the physician or nurse practitioner must have comprehensive knowledge in order to make informed decisions for his or her patients. Often with differing shifts and hospital and office locations, there is a breakdown in how data is processed, as well as how it is protected.

This past year marked the debut of A-Space (Analytic Space), touted as the "MySpace for Agents" in the media, and perhaps a desirable set of collaborative tools for health care—one that may prove far more beneficial than the clipboard. The networking site is for agents and analysts within the 16 U.S. Intelligence agencies. Electronic workspace is provided in order to access interagency databases and sources, along with Web-based messaging and other collaborative tools. Andrew McAfee of the Harvard Business School calls it "a means of sharing information that in the normal course of events might not be seen at all" (McAfee, 2008). Mark Granovetter, a sociologist and author of *The Strength of Weak Ties*, also referred to as SWT, suggests that "A-Space encourages collaboration among people with weak ties." It strengthens the weakness. This ideology is also notable in SWOT (Strengths, Weaknesses, Opportunities, and Threats) analysis and the TOWS (a variant order of SWOT) matrix in which specific strategies are developed. This is a strategic management tool we, the authors, implemented for the technology division of the FBI at headquarters in Washington, D.C. and at Fort Monmouth, New Jersey. A similar plan could be developed by and for stakeholders within the health care community.

One suggestion for protecting patient privacy is to emulate an adjustment to the model used in law enforcement: "Role-based templates" that are "specific to the job, rather than the person." These templates would provide clearances to position profiles in advance of the choice of individuals. This would provide for a timely transition in a field that holds a high turnover of part-time positions, with emergency room physicians given the highest level of access. "If someone leaves and a new hire takes over, the role-based template applies to the new person in that position; it does not have to be recreated" (Wagley, 2008).

Certainly, technology management, security experts, health professionals, and patient rights activists will be monitoring the implementation of this plan with interest and analysis.

Article: Your private health details may already be online

By Elizabeth Cohen
June 5, 2008
CNN

ATLANTA, Georgia—Imagine my surprise when, in the course of doing research for this story, I stumbled upon my own personal health information online.

There it was in black, white, and hypertext blue. My annual mammograms; the visits to the podiatrist for the splinter in my foot; the kind of birth control I use—it was all on my health insurance company's Web site. And that's not all: The prescriptions drugs I use were listed on the Web site where I get my prescription drug insurance.

I had no idea this was all on the World Wide Web. Welcome to the 21st century, says Dr. Steven Schwaitzberg, associate professor of surgery at Harvard Medical School and a medical informatics expert.

"There's more information out there about people than could ever possibly be realized," he says.

Yes, indeed. Every diagnosis, treatment, and doctor's appointment I'd had since 2003 was on the Internet. All I needed to get them was a phone call to my insurance company and information other people might know, such as my Social Security number, date of birth and address. Someone's spouse in the middle of a divorce could try to access personal health information. An employer could try to do the same. And what about hackers? If a 17-year-old can hack into an iPhone, couldn't someone just as clever get into my insurance company's Web site?

Should I try to get my health information off the Internet? Or maybe I should be glad it's there—perhaps it could be helpful to me in some way. As electronic medical records become more and more common, here are five questions we all need to ask.

1. What are the advantages to having your health information online?

If your health records are online, you can, to some extent, double-check your doctor. In a world where physicians are busy and medical errors are epidemic, that's no small thing.

Here's one example: Two years ago, Dr. Jim Jirjis CQ ordered a CT scan for his patient Doug Smith, who was having searing chest pain. Jirjis heard from the radiologist that Smith's heart was just fine.

"I was relieved and immediately called him on the telephone and said, 'Great news,' " says Jirjis, an internist at Vanderbilt University Medical Center in Nashville, Tennessee.

Thanks to Vanderbilt's online medical records, Doug could read the CT scan report himself. Several pages in, he saw something Jirjis hadn't: The radiologist had noticed a lesion on the right side of his thyroid.

That lesion turned out to be cancer. It was caught early, when it could be treated easily. "Online records empower the patients," Jirjis says. "Most physicians are reviewing an enormous amount of lab results every day. The patient is reviewing just one person's lab results."

Another advantage to online records is that they travel with you. Let's say you become ill while on vacation and can't remember the name of every medication you take, or your exact diagnoses. Just get to a computer and the out-of-town doctor has your records instantly.

"Having medical records online helps me take better care of you, and helps you take better care of yourself," says Dr. Daniel Sands, an assistant clinical professor of medicine at Harvard Medical School and senior medical informatics director at Cisco.

2. What are the disadvantages?

Electronic health information enthusiasts, like Sands, still have concerns about privacy. "Absolutely, there are risks associated with online medical records," he says.

Online health Web sites are "https" secure sites and password protected, but is it 100 percent secure?

No, says Amanda Angelotti, a spokeswoman for Google Health, a recently launched site where users can store their health information.

"In some sense, no one can ever really know about the data they hand over, whether it's financial data or medical data or anything else," Angelotti says. "In some sense you can never be truly protected. But if we can't protect people's personal information, they wouldn't trust us and use our products."

Google's privacy policy states the company doesn't sell user health information, and doesn't share with others unless the user explicitly authorizes it (one exception is if there's a court order or subpoena to hand information over).

Microsoft has a similar service called HealthVault. On the site, the company says it may disclose a user's personal information to comply with the law, to protect the "personal safety" of members of the public, or to defend the rights of Microsoft."

It adds that it uses "a variety of security technologies and procedures to help protect your personal information from unauthorized access."

3. If your medical information is already online, can you make it disappear?

If your health insurance company, or your healthcare provider, put your information online and you don't want it there, it's worth asking if they can take it off.

I found out I can get my health information from my insurance company's Web site (although it wasn't obvious how; they had to show me). At Cambridge Health Alliance in Massachusetts, where Schwaitzberg is chief of surgery, members can also opt out of online health records.

Before you do that, though, find out what's online—it might not be as revealing as you think. For example, my insurance company says it doesn't include information about substance abuse, mental health, sexually transmitted diseases, or "sensitive issues around reproductive health."

4. Should you put your health information online with a service like Google Health or Microsoft HealthVault?

If you like the idea of electronic medical records, you can create your own at Google Health, Microsoft HealthVault, or other Web sites.

If you, like many people, still have paper medical records, you can have them scanned into an electronic record. There are various ways to do this, some at a cost of $15 to $150.

Sands advises everyone to ask specific questions before signing up. "You really have to read the fine print," he says. "You need to ask, 'Who other than me will have access to this information? Will there be an audit trail—a list of who else has seen this information?' " he says.

If you do decide to build your own electronic medical record, Schwaitzberg says to put in only information "you wouldn't mind reading on the front page of your local newspaper."

"My white cell count, my potassium levels, aren't very interesting, so I don't mind having them in an electronic record," Schwaitzberg says. "But DNA test results showing I had a propensity for cancer might be interesting to someone, like an insurer or a future employer."

5. What's the best way to use your online medical records?

Making the most out of your medical records will require some work. While some information is relatively easy to understand (like Doug Smith's lesion on his thyroid), other information is confusing "medspeak."

Group Health, a health care system based in Seattle, Washington, offers the Healthwise Knowledgebase to its patients. Accessible to anyone, it has definitions of various diagnoses, medications, and medical tests.

The Medical Library Association offers a "deciphering medspeak" glossary, and a list of commonly used medical abbreviations. Labtestsonline has an A–Z guide to common medical tests.

Things to Think About

1. Several public advocacy groups and industry giants have joined to make recommendations to Congress to create new federal privacy legislation (McMilan, 2009). This group believes that consumer consent is not understood and should be made easier. One member of the group stated, "My mom doesn't know what an IP address is." Is this an unfair burden to the consumer?

2. There are 38 state laws covering data breach notification. Since many of these state laws are different, does it make sense to standardize them under one federal law?

3. Congress passed the 1996 Health Insurance Portability and Accountability Act (HIPAA). Should such a law exist to protect consumer privacy in general? What does HIPAA cover?

4. Some health insurance plans would like to see data breach notification only when the breach is determined to have harmful effects. Do you believe this violates the rights of patients?

5. *PC World* reported on Michael Stokes, principal program manager in the company's Health Solutions Group, explaining his position on the special nature of health data. "Health data is often considered more sensitive than other personally identifiable information," he said. Explain.

Key Terms

1. Google Health

2. Microsoft HealthVault

FORUM 12
Network Vulnerabilities: Script Kiddies

❝Anatomy of a Subway Hack" was the name of the presentation to be given by three MIT students who figured out a way to evade the Massachusetts Bay Transportation Authority's (MBTA) computer security system and change a $1.25 fare card to a $100 fare card. The MBTA, however, sought a temporary court injunction to stop the three hackers from speaking at DEFCON, a popular Las Vegas hackers' convention, in order to prevent public knowledge of its security flaws. Their professors and other leading scientists defended the students, arguing that the injunction could have a dangerous impact on computer security research (Heussner, 2008).

If only student hackers could always be so helpful! What about the student hackers who create havoc for educational institutions?

In 2007, two students at California State University were placed on felony probation for changing grades for cash (Leyden, 2007). That same year, two high school students provided a fake snow day in Trenton, Ohio, after hacking into their school's computer system (NBC News, 2007). In 2008, two Orange County teenagers made headlines as they were accused of hacking in order to steal exams and change grades, with one student charged with 69 felony counts (Martindale, 2008). That same year, a Broward County, Florida, teenager was accused of hacking into his high school computer and downloading a database of personnel information (Sun Sentinel, 2008). In 2009, hackers targeted 20 elementary schools in the U.K., placing pornography on their Web sites (Telegraph, 2009).

The list goes on. These represent just a few of the headlines that have appeared across the globe in recent years. Hacking into school computer systems is a pervasive and expensive problem for school districts and law enforcement. Among other problems, it often creates data breaches that are useful to identity thieves. What strategies have been implemented that can prevent such occurrences?

Article: Getting a grasp on student hackers

By Dennis Carter
July 15, 2008
eSchoolNews

School IT administrators know that some students will do anything to breach network security systems designed to block inappropriate web sites and keep students on task. When a group of school district IT chiefs met recently to discuss the challenges of reining in students armed with tech savvy and a determination to wreak network havoc, their tales were cautionary—but their advice could prove valuable as computers become more common in K-12 schools.

Nearly a dozen school network administrators met July 1 at the National Education Computing Conference (NECC) in San Antonio, where thousands of educators from across the country came to see the latest in classroom technology. During a breakfast meeting, school district IT chiefs suggested recruiting students to help expose network vulnerabilities and warned of a new threat to campus computer security: "war driving."

Lloyd Brown, director of technology and information services for Virginia's Henrico County Public Schools, said tech-savvy students in his district recently rallied a group of 30 peers to meet in the quad during their school's lunch break. Sitting side by side, the students continuously hit the F5 key on their laptops, which refreshes a web page— devouring the school's internet bandwidth—and eventually broke through the school system's network filter, allowing students to view pornographic web sites. School IT officials from across the county were concerned about the security breach, Brown said, because laptops are becoming more commonplace—especially in high schools.

Searching for a quick solution, Brown met with officials from 8e6 Technologies, a company that provides internet filtering and reporting solutions for school systems nationwide, and found a fix: Henrico would maintain a detailed log of computers that attempted to view "blocked" web pages. Once the action was logged, that computer's internet connection was cut off, and school administrators could take disciplinary action against students who tried to subvert the network and its security measures.

This tactic cut down on incidents of student hacking, but Brown said he wanted to recruit students smart enough to find ways around the school system's comprehensive security package. After eight students were suspended for 10 days for violating the district's acceptable-use rules, Brown hired the group and had them work part-time with district IT employees. The students were charged with "finding the weak spots" in Henrico's network. Once district IT officials saw how students worked their way around the periphery of the network, they quickly made alterations—eliminating vulnerabilities that were being exposed by an increasing number of students.

"They love the status," Brown said when asked how the students reacted when school officials offered them a part-time gig. "They try to figure out where the holes are, and it really helps us."

Shielding students from web sites that could distract from daily lessons has paid off for Henrico County: A study recently released by the school district showed that students who used their laptops the most scored higher in several subjects, including biology and chemistry, although they scored lower in algebra and writing classes. (See "Study: Laptop learning is improving for Henrico students.")

The data were part of a three-year study that aims to show whether, and how, students and teachers in Henrico County use laptops effectively in the classroom. Researchers noted significant improvement among teachers in incorporating laptops into everyday lessons during year two of the study. The study's first year showed a widespread failure to use the 21st-century tools for students' benefit.

Jim Culbert, who has served as chief information officer for the Duval County Schools in Jacksonville, Fla., since 1998, told his fellow school IT chiefs about his experience with an eighth grader who was determined to find his way through the district's network security.

The boy, 13, whom Culbert described as "underprivileged," did not have a computer at home. His only interaction with computers was at school, where he often stayed late to become proficient on the web. The student eventually taught himself how to level devastating proxy attacks on the school district's security system, giving Culbert and his IT staff headaches as they tried to counter the attacks. Culbert said the student was suspended for five days, but when the boy returned to school, Culbert said he was so impressed by the youth's willingness to learn about computers that he took him in and had him coached by IT staff.

This wasn't the first time Culbert encountered acceptable-use violations on school system computer equipment. In 2006, Culbert briefed the Duval County School Board on a rash of students and faculty who used school equipment to view pornography online. Board members asked Culbert to shore up the network, and with products from 8e6 Technologies, IT personnel soon were able to track users' web use—knowing when a student or faculty member was viewing inappropriate web sites using school equipment.

Several school district IT managers at the NECC meeting were concerned about the trend of linking pornographic web sites to popular blogs visited daily by students. The blog web pages are not blocked, tech chiefs said, because they are not usually included on a school system's list of prohibited web sites. But many blogs—even if they are not related to pornographic material—include a host of web links that transfer students directly to porn sites, among others, which often damage a network and clog a district's bandwidth.

School tech chiefs said they feared a student backlash if their favorite non-pornographic web sites were blocked. They added that as more sites include porn links, many sites that were once accessible to students and staff would be blocked accidentally. But as web filtering becomes more sophisticated, network security tools will be able to weed out only the sites that violate strict acceptable-use rules laid out every school year, 8e6 officials said.

School tech administrators and 8e6 President Paul Myer also discussed a recent trend in student hacking, known popularly as "war driving," or finding and documenting vulnerabilities in Wi-Fi networks. War-driving software is readily available on the internet, such as NetStumbler for Windows or SWScanner for Linux—posing a constant worry for school IT directors.

Students nationwide have stalked in and around their schools, searching for unsecured wireless access points from which they can view web sites that are usually blocked by the district's filtering system. When these access points are discovered—most often near the edges of a school's campus—students make a mark on a nearby tree or sidewalk, signaling to other students where they can avoid network security.

Myer said this phenomenon is complicating efforts to provide students with school-issued laptops, known as one-to-one computing initiatives.

"It is a real problem" for one-to-one initiatives, Myer said.

The breakfast meeting ended with a discussion about recovering stolen laptop computers. While network security is an IT administrator's foremost responsibility, some officials said stolen Mac laptops are always recovered. When a police report is filed by a Mac owner, a camera imbedded in the computer snaps pictures of the perpetrator. One IT chief who did not want to be identified said his school had recovered "100 percent" of the laptops stolen from faculty and staff.

Things to Think About

1. In the movie, "Catch Me If You Can," Leonardo DiCaprio played a real check forger named Frank Abagnale, Jr., who was later employed by financial institutions to investigate fraud. Do you think schools who enlist malicious hackers (crackers) are acting ethically?

2. Today, Frank Abagnale, Jr. lives in the Midwestern part of the United States and continues to work to combat fraud. It has been reported that he earns millions of dollars employed in this profession. Are there ethical concerns for this outcome?

3. What do you believe contributed to Frank's decision to engage in criminal activity? What would you consider to be contributing factors toward Frank's rehabilitation?

4. List strategies schools could employ to minimize hacking before it occurs. Beyond the use of firewalls and other such implementations, what plan for education might also be effective?

5. How can education and industry fight the emergence of war driving? Should home users have the same concerns?

Key Terms

1. War driving

2. Bandwidth

FORUM 13
Copyright Protection and the Electronic Textbook

"Internet piracy trial of the decade," is what some have labeled the trial of February 2009, in which the owners of *The Pirate Bay* Web site were accused of facilitating illegal downloads of copyrighted material. Some argue that because *The Pirate Bay* and other sites like it merely point to illegal content, rather than hold it on their sites, they should not be held liable for breaking copyright law (Harvey, 2009).

The Pirate Bay, located in Sweden, indexes and tracks BitTorrent files and is considered the world's largest BitTorrent tracker. BitTorrent is an open source, peer-to-peer, data sharing protocol that is used to transfer large files (see http://www.bittorrent.com). But *The Pirate Bay* is not alone. *Textbook Torrents* promises thousands of textbooks to be downloaded in PDF (portable document format) for those willing to risk a different kind of "booking." Now, the Association of American Publishers (AAP) has strengthened efforts to enforce copyright laws by monitoring instances of illegal downloading of textbooks by college students on these sites and others.

Who are these students? Gay Gaddis, CEO of the T3 advertising agency, refers to students today as Generation Now (Gaddis, 2006). They are described as a "culture of immediacy" as they have grown up highly connected to communication and media technologies. Thus, they are active consumers. They are college freshmen who, according to one study, spent $8.2 billion on technology during the back-to-school shopping season (Fetterman, 2006). Digital students are not only comfortable with textbooks that are electronic, but also pleased by the opportunity to acquire books electronically.

However, in the scope of all other digital expenditures, some ask why the digital generation risks viable lawsuits to pilfer the intellectual property of authors and publishers. Does "why" even matter? Most assuredly, it appears that the AAP will be as easily recognizable as the Recording Industry Association of America (RIAA).

If judges feel the same level of frustration as members of Congress, violators beware! Representative Howard Berman is reported to have jokingly stated that he "probably does not favor the death penalty for infringers" (Goldman, 2003).

Did a teacher ever remind you that "many a truth is said in jest"? Some believe that his statement speaks volumes (pun intended).

Article: Copyright fight looms over college textbooks

By Maya T. Prabhu
July 25, 2008
eSchool News

The high cost of college textbooks has spawned a new battleground in the fight to keep students from downloading copyright-protected materials over the internet: textbook file sharing.

Several web sites allow—and, in some cases, encourage—students to make available scanned copies of textbook pages for others to download free of charge, often using the same peer-to-peer file-sharing technology that is used to swap music and movies online.

"In the age of Napster and peer-to-peer file sharing for music, young people are used to taking copyrighted material," said J.D. Harriman, a partner in the intellectual property practice for the Los Angeles-based law firm DLA Piper. "This is not the education we want to give these students from the very beginning—to be copyright infringers."

Driving this latest trend are soaring textbook prices, which have risen at twice the annual rate of inflation over the last 20 years, a study done by the Government Accountability Office has found.

According to the College Board, the average college student spent between $805 and $1,229 on books and supplies alone during the 2007-08 school year. In the National Association of College Stores' 2008 Student Watch Survey of Student Attitudes & Buying Habits, students surveyed estimated they spent $702 on required course materials annually. Required Course Materials include: printed texts (both new and used), electronic textbooks, and course packs and customized materials.

And though pressure from educational publishers prompted the host of a major textbook-sharing web site to pull the plug on its service earlier this month, legal experts say that's just the beginning of what could become a protracted campaign by the publishing industry to end the sharing of copyrighted texts online—much as the recording industry has tried to do with music file-sharing on college campuses.

So far, publishers have limited their efforts to targeting offending web sites, similar to how the recording industry tried to shut down Napster and other music-sharing web sites earlier this decade.

But if the campaign to curb textbook file-sharing follows the same arc as that of the music industry's efforts, it's possible this movement could shift its focus onto the students themselves who download or make available copyrighted texts online—especially as publishers realize how hard it is to keep up with an ever-changing lineup of textbook-sharing web sites.

After more than a year of enabling students to scan, share, and download textbook content online, free of charge, Textbook Torrent—the largest and most high-profile of these textbook-sharing web sites—was no longer online as of press time.

Textbook Torrent reportedly offered more than 5,000 textbooks for downloading in PDF format, complete with their original layout and full-color illustrations. Users of the site could download and share these documents in the same fashion that music and movies have been shared in the past—through the peer-to-peer file-sharing system BitTorrent.

In June, Pearson Education requested that Textbook Torrent remove 78 of the company's titles from the site, and the site administrator complied. Then, earlier this month, the site disappeared from the web altogether.

Students and other web users who go to www.textbooktorrent.com are now redirected to www.totalcampus.com, a web site containing nothing more than a link to Amazon.com's portal for buying and selling new and used textbooks online.

But that might not be the end of the web site for good. An internet search for "Textbook Torrent" turned up an archived web page with the following message:

"I have some more bad news for you: we've had our server pulled out from under us. Call it a 'personality conflict' with our former new host—apparently they're not too happy with hosting a BitTorrent tracker, particularly one that has has [sic] been getting so much recognition of late. The *good* news is that all sensitive information has been securely erased from the server and we were able to back everything up, supplementing our automatic daily backups. What's more, thanks to a generous offer from a fellow tracker administrator, we will be rooming with another tracker until we can find more permanent accomodations [sic].

"Choosing a server in the U.S. was a mistake, and I should have known better. I'm sorry for that. We will be moving to a more permanent server prior to the August/September rush, so be ready for that.... In the meantime, please turn DHT/peer sharing on in your BitTorrent clients, which should keep your torrents ticking along nicely....

"That's all for now, folks. I'll keep you posted. **We will be back soon**. C'mon, people. It's not the end of the world."

Ed McCoyd, director of digital policy at the Association of American Publishers (AAP), released a statement July 22 noting that textbook publishers are actively enforcing their copyrights. The organization hired an outside law firm earlier this summer to search the internet for textbooks that are being offered illegally.

"AAP is vigilant in searching for copyright violations, and when sites are found that infringe, no matter the genre, the association and publishers will notify web site operators and internet service providers about the infringements and request that they be immediately removed. This has proven to be an effective approach," McCoyd said.

In February, Pearson Education—along with McGraw-Hill Education, John Wiley & Sons Inc., and Cengage Learning Inc. (formerly Thomson Learning)—settled a trademark and copyright infringement lawsuit against the owner and operator of ValoreBooks.com.

The lawsuit alleged that the site enabled sales of pirated educational materials and foreign manufactured editions of textbooks that were not authorized for sale in North America. As part of the settlement, ValoreBooks was prohibited from selling and distributing any pirated electronic copies of the publishers' works.

"The complaint against Valore and this settlement underscore the firm commitment by these publishers to protect their own intellectual property rights and the rights of their author," Ronald G. Dove Jr., an attorney representing the publishers, said in a press release.

"Businesses and individuals should know that the publishers will continue to pursue legal action against those who violate their intellectual property rights, including those web site operators who may not themselves directly infringe the publishers' rights, but who provide internet marketplaces that permit and assist others in doing so."

Web sites such as Scribd and Demonoid also enable users to upload and share many types of files—and a search of these sites revealed several copyrighted textbooks as of press time.

One user on Demonoid was offering 50 architecture books, including copyrighted titles such as *Assessing Building Performance and Modern Bamboo Architecture*, in one torrent. Another user was offering several math, science, and engineering textbooks, such as *Quantum Mechanics for Scientists and Engineers* and *How Math Explains the World*.

Scribed, a free, web-based document sharing community and self-publishing platform, enables anyone to publish, distribute, share, and discover documents of all kinds. All a user has to do is sign up for a free account and provide an eMail address.

Scribd appears to take copyrights seriously; it has a section that reads, in part: "It is our policy to respond to clear notices of alleged copyright infringement that comply with the Digital Millennium Copyright Act. In addition, we will promptly terminate without notice the accounts of those determined by us to be 'repeat infringers.'"

Even so, a quick search of Scribd using the term "textbook" revealed at least a few copyrighted works—including all 2,227 pages of *Brunner & Suddarth's Textbook of Medical-Surgical Nursing, 10th edition*, which had been viewed 1,075 time as of press time.

Scribd spokesman Jason Bentley said there is no way, either technically or practically, to guarantee that copyrighted material is never uploaded or shared online. But, besides promptly removing copyrighted materials that are called to its attention, Scribd also uses an automated copyright filter that searches each file as it is uploaded for key words that could indicate a copyright violation.

"The filter is still in beta, but improves every day," Bentley said.

Soaring textbook costs haven't just spawned a new illicit trade—they've also encouraged a movement toward using free and open textbooks on campus.

Open Text Book, run by the Open Knowledge Foundation, is an online registry of textbooks and related materials that are free for anyone to use and distribute through a Creative Commons license or similar agreement.

Besides serving as an online repository for free and open textbooks, the site also links to other open-textbook initiatives, such as the California Open-Source Textbook Project, the Free Textbook Project, Rice University's Connexions project (see "Rice builds body of knowledge"), and Wikibooks.

This fall, a start-up enterprise called Flat World Knowledge will conduct what it calls "the nation's largest test of open college textbooks." The nationwide beta test involves hundreds of students from 15 colleges and universities, who will use Flat World's free and open textbooks in a single class or section at each school. The beta test begins next month and will run through the end of the fall semester, Flat World said.

"The traditional textbook publishing model no longer serves the interests of students, educators, and authors," said Jeff Shelstad, co-founder and CEO of Flat World Knowledge and former editorial director for Prentice Hall's business publishing division.

"Textbooks are too expensive for students and too inflexible for instructors," Shelstad said. "And authors—the major, initial source of value in the industry—are increasingly confused by faster revision demands and their compensation for those revisions. Flat World addresses all of these industry pain points."

Flat World's books will be open for faculty to customize and available to students free of charge online. Flat World and its authors will earn their money by offering supplemental materials to students beyond the free online book—from printed, on-demand textbooks for around $30, to audio books for around $25, to downloadable and printable files by chapter. The company also will sell low-priced study aids, such as podcast study guides, digital flash cards, and interactive practice quizzes.

Of course, open textbooks will be successful only if colleges and their faculty choose to use them instead of pricier, more traditional options.

Toward this end, the Student Public Interest Research Groups, a nonprofit student advocacy network, has been pushing for open textbooks since 2003, *USA Today* reports.

The groups' Make Textbooks Affordable campaign has been gathering signatures for an Open Textbook Statement of Intent, which asks faculty to consider using open textbooks. As of press time, the statement reportedly had collected more than 1,200 signatures from college faculty in all 50 states.

Meanwhile, Scribd's Bentley offered a bit of advice for students.

"The big publishers are far less interested in addressing the root causes of textbook piracy—such as egregious cost—than they are in finding out who you are and making an example out of you," he said.

"Do not assume that, because you have an electronic version of a textbook, it's OK to share it on the internet. Save your sob stories about how you came from a single-parent, blue-collar family on loans and how one required textbook costs more than your rent and food budget combined. That's not the point.... Don't share your textbooks."

Things to Think About

1. What did you think about Bentley's advice to students? Is he behaving ethically by informing those who appear ignorant to the law of the serious repercussions in the future?

2. What can the AAP learn from the RIAA? Research civil suits brought about by the RIAA.

3. Some members of Congress have suggested stronger penalties for copyright infringement. Has the temperament of Congress changed? Will stronger penalties deter piracy?

4. One growing problem is the use of the BitTorrent protocol, a program used for downloading large files that is widely used on illegal peer-to-peer networks. Would dismantling the network sites serve as a viable response? What are the obstacles to this approach?

5. Is there a system that could be put in place that may serve to minimize textbook piracy, similar to how the iPod's entrance to the marketplace appeared to help reduce music piracy? Explain how the iPod appeared to assist in reducing music piracy.

Key Terms

1. AAP

2. BitTorrent protocol

FORUM 14
Wireless Mobile Computing

Imagine if the United States Federal Communications Commission (FCC) considered using white space, the unused portions of television airwaves, to provide free broadband service to every American. After all, taxpayers recently spent millions on an effort to transition from analog to digital broadcasting that would provide the potential for additional white space—space that might be used for this and other purposes. Complicating matters is that the National Association of Broadcasters (NAB) has come out against the proposal on the basis of technical inadequacies. The government expects the plan to work and industry expects the plan to fail. What's a nation to do?

Article: National Wi-Fi plan moves one step closer: Phone giant opposes FCC's push for free wireless broadband

October 21, 2008
eSchool News

The Federal Communications Commission (FCC) said on Oct. 10 the agency's plans to provide free national broadband internet access will not cause significant interference with phone companies' networks, but at least one wireless carrier disagrees.

Phone company T-Mobile has warned in recent months that the FCC's plans to bring free Wi-Fi to the United States could interfere with certain frequencies on the company's $4 billion Advanced Wireless Services-1 spectrum.

The FCC rebutted these claims in a report, which said the nationwide Wi-Fi network would "not necessarily result in interference." The agency's report brings the promise of a nationwide wireless broadband network one step closer to reality.

T-Mobile officials said they want the FCC to reevaluate the plan and open the proposal to public comment once again.

"A reasonable comment period would give the public a chance to review those conclusions before the Commission acts in reliance on them," Thomas Sugrue, the company's vice president of government affairs, wrote to the FCC.

The FCC is expected to unveil rules for the free Wi-Fi network by the end of the year. Parts of the new spectrum could be auctioned off in 2009, officials said. Under FCC guidelines, companies that win the spectrum would be forced to filter adult content and cover 95 percent of the U.S. population in the next decade.

Meanwhile, FCC Chairman Kevin Martin announced Oct. 15 that the agency is considering using unused portions of television airwaves—known as "white space"—for broadband service.

Martin's proposal appeals to public interest groups and many of the nation's biggest technology companies, including Google Inc. and Microsoft Corp., which hope it will bring affordable, high-speed internet connections to more Americans.

"No one should ever underestimate the potential that new technologies and innovations may bring to society," Martin said in a statement.

Shure Inc., a manufacturer of wireless microphones, has also raised concerns about interference with audio systems at concerts and sporting events.

Martin issued his proposal ahead of the official release of a technical report by FCC engineers concluding that potential interference could be eliminated with the use of wireless transmitter devices that rely on spectrum-sensing and "geo-location" technologies to detect and avoid nearby broadcast signals.

Martin, one of three Republicans on the five-member FCC, circulated his proposal to his colleagues ahead of a Nov. 4 vote on the plan. He wants to allow the use of white spaces to provide broadband following the upcoming transition from analog to digital TV broadcasting in February, which will free up additional parts of the wireless spectrum. That space could be used to deliver high-speed internet connections as well as improved communications networks to connect police officers, fire fighters, and other emergency responders.

The National Association of Broadcasters (NAB) quickly came out against the FCC's white space proposal. The groups said some tests conducted by FCC engineers caused wireless devices to malfunction. Seventy members of Congress have also expressed concern over the fallout from using white space.

"It would appear that the FCC is misinterpreting the actual data collected by their own engineers," said NAB Executive Vice President Dennis Wharton, adding that the FCC's 149-page report "raises troubling questions."

Supporters of the plan say the vacant spaces between television channels are particularly well suited to providing broadband since they can penetrate walls, carry a great deal of data, and reach a wide geographic area.

"Freeing up these powerful airwaves will create a boom in innovative technologies and expand the opportunities for citizens to communicate with one another and the rest of the world," said Ben Scott, policy director for the advocacy group Free Press.

Scott Blake Harris, counsel to the White Spaces Coalition, added that harnessing white spaces will create a multibillion market for advanced wireless devices to transmit and receive signals, including laptops, personal digital assistants, and set-top boxes. Members of the White Spaces Coalition include Microsoft, Google, Dell Inc., Hewlett-Packard Co., and Phillips Electronics.

Martin's white space proposal is one of several in which he is pushing to use wireless technology to bring affordable broadband to parts of the country that lack high-speed internet service. He also wants to require telecommunications carriers to use the Universal Service fund, which subsidizes phone service in underserved areas, to invest in broadband.

Things to Think About

1. What is the gist of T-Mobile's argument against a national Wi-Fi plan? What are the arguments involved in using television white space for Wi-Fi?

2. Discuss ways the economy might benefit from extensive low-cost broadband service.

3. Are there any economic or social risks involved in providing broadband service to a nation's population at no charge? Is there evidence that this has been properly implemented elsewhere?

4. Could the opinion of the National Association of Broadcasters represent a conflict of interest? If so, how could this be overcome?

5. What suggestions would you make for going forward? How could the SDLC be implemented to assist in this plan?

Key Terms

1. White space

2. Geolocation technologies

FORUM 15
Information Overload

Need an ice breaker? Just bring up information overload and the room will be buzzing in seconds. It seems that almost every professional I know has a personal story to share about how this has impacted the quality of his or her life. In fact, another term roaming around cyberspace that may better describe this problem is *information asphyxiation*! It is increasingly cited as a concern that appears to diminish workplace efficiency.

While struggling to find the time to respond to electronic communication is not a recent phenomenon, the obstacles created by it now appear to have been exacerbated by the onslaught of Web 2.0 software. Betsy Schiffman, a technology author, contends that these programs have done more than foster communication; they have led to information overload and "possibly a nasty internet addiction." He describes Twitter and Facebook as "torture by information overload" (Schiffman, 2008).

Not surprisingly, new software has been developed to deal with the problem. Xobni is described as an artificial intelligence-equipped email monitor that plugs into Outlook and helps the user organize, search, and navigate his or her email. It will identify the times of the day when the user receives the most important email, for example. ClearContext identifies the user's most valued contacts, flags messages, and provides an enhanced sorter (Hendrickson, 2008).

If more software doesn't sound like the answer, email-free Fridays might. This began among engineers at Intel and spread to U.S. Cellular as a means to control the flow of emails and better connect with colleagues. It also sends a message to the organization that may change the culture; that is, email is not welcome unless it is really necessary.

Article: Buried in eMail? Try these six tips to dig out

October 21, 2008
eSchool News

"You've got mail!" Remember when that alert sounded thrilling?

Today, not so much.

As scores of electronic messages pour into school eMail in-boxes and spill onto cell phones and handheld devices, the flood often leaves teachers and administrators feeling overwhelmed. But take heart. In just a moment, you'll learn six strategies experts say will put you back in control of your eMail and rescue your endangered productivity.

"We're like frazzled lab rats, being poked and prodded and beeped and pinged," says Maggie Jackson, author of *Distracted: The Erosion of Attention and the Coming Dark Age*.

The average employee in the United States receives 200 eMail messages a day, according to the business and technology research firm Basex in its report "Information Overload: We Have Met the Enemy and He Is Us."

It's an unfortunate irony that a system once lauded for its promises of efficiency has filled hours on the job with wasted, fragmented time.

Basex found that eMail correspondence and other interruptions decrease productivity for U.S. companies at a cost of more than $650 billion per year for billions of lost staff hours. For school employees, more time spent keeping up with eMail means less time focused on teaching and learning.

Constant access to information, communication, and technology has become such a big issue, experts say, that its implications go beyond a lack of productivity and focus at work. eMail and information overload also eats into the quality of relationships both at school and at home.

"Attention is the bedrock to learning, memory, social connection, and happiness," Jackson says.

And yet, at many schools and businesses, a culture is developing that rewards immediacy over focus, so that attending to what's new at any given moment takes precedence over long-term goals. The result? A series of interruptions, such as eMail, that get in the way of the big-picture goals.

"eMail is being used like a drug to get a hit of accomplishment when one feels he is spinning his wheels," says technology analyst Craig Roth in his blog, KnowledgeForward.

In July, technology companies and other industry experts launched the non-profit Information Overload Research Group. Its mission: Raise awareness of how current communication tools can impede productivity.

And the industry that created this problem is also trying to capitalize by helping people organize their in-boxes.

A program called C-MAIL promises to help prioritize eMail by learning through the user's clicks about what is more or less important.

The makers of Xobni, which is "inbox" spelled backwards, say their Microsoft Outlook plug-in speeds up the process by "threading" conversations, or grouping responses together.

Productivity gurus also have created a cottage industry out of eMail overload. Here's a sampling of their advice:

(1) Don't check eMail when you first start work. Experts say you should take care of an important task first before checking eMail, so that you don't use eMail as an excuse for postponing more pressing obligations.

(2) Check eMail in batches, rather than fluidly throughout the day. Some experts suggest checking eMail twice a day; others, up to five times. But the important thing is efficiency.

"You wouldn't do a new load of laundry every time you have a dirty pair of socks," says Timothy Ferriss, author of The 4-Hour Workweek.

(3) Minimize exchanges. "Learn to propose, instead of asking questions," Ferriss says. Instead of asking what time a person can meet for lunch, just jump right in and propose a few times. You can use "if, then" language, such as: "If you can't meet at 11, how about 12?"

(4) Limit sending eMail. Sending less eMail means receiving less eMail, and sending shorter messages will garner shorter responses.

"This does not mean that you should write elliptically or bypass standard grammar, capitalization, and punctuation," says Merlin Mann on his productivity blog 43 Folders, "just that your well-written message can, and should, be as concise as possible."

(5) Take it to zero. In an extreme case, some experts suggest wiping your in-box completely away and starting fresh. You can always send your contacts a message telling them what you've done, and asking them to resend any truly important messages.

(6) Use other forms of communication. eMail has earned a solid place in the workplace, but in some cases it's not the most appropriate form of communication.

"When you're overusing it for the petty things, like [contacting] the guy in the next cubicle, stand up and ask him the question," says Cherie Kerr, author of The Bliss or 'Diss' Connection: eMail Etiquette for the Business Professional.

She suggests picking up the phone if an eMail thread gets longer than three back-and-forths.

"I don't care how many pieces of technology we have," she says. "At the end of the day, it's always going to be about relationships."

Things to Think About

1. Research is compelling that it takes us approximately 4 minutes to return to our work with the same level of thought processes whenever we are interrupted or distracted. Is it possible to process information or data when interruption is fairly constant?

2. Have you ever received an email that looked something like this? "FW: FWD>FWD-(FWD) a joke for…" How do you feel about receiving many personal emails among your email for work? What policies, if any, would you have in your firm to deal with this kind of email?

3. The article suggests that email does not nurture relationships. Do you agree? How could this be avoided?

4. Is voicemail still really necessary? If so, under what conditions?

5. How can voicemail messages be saved with email messages to save time in "hearing" messages?

Key Terms

1. Fragmented time

2. C-MAIL

FORUM 16
Technology Literacy

Thomas Kurtz, a professor at Dartmouth and co-developer of the BASIC computer language, once asked a question that is often quoted by information technology professionals. In 1964, he said, "How can managers make effective decisions about computing and its uses, when they are essentially ignorant of it?" His message is still an important reminder today. Since every manager, whether a teacher, a minister, or a CEO, will need to partake in decisions that involve the use of technology in his or her organization, he or she ought to be competent to do so.

In 1999, a study funded by the National Science Foundation was developed by the National Research Council, a non-profit institution that provides independent advice on science and technology issues under congressional charter. The report on technology literacy was entitled *Being Fluent with Information Technology* and is available in full text for free on the Web (http://www.nap.edu/openbook.php?record_id=6482). It stated that there are three essential and interrelated components for using information technology effectively, and that these provide a framework to build fluency in information technology. They are (1) intellectual capabilities, the application and interpretation of computer concepts and skills used in problem solving; (2) concepts, the fundamental ideas and processes that support information technology such as how information is represented digitally; and (3) skills, abilities that are associated with particular hardware and software systems (CSTB, 1999).

The executive summary of the National Research Council's committee said, "There is concern on the part of some citizens that changes implied by information technology embody potential risks to social values, freedoms or economic interests, etc., obligating them to be informed" (CSTB, 1999).

Could you imagine driving a car without understanding the road signs, knowing the laws, and recognizing the risks? Do you think that there are actually people who use computers who do so without such a basic understanding?

Article: On the way: Nation's first tech-literacy exam— Tech literacy to be added to Nation's Report Card beginning in 2012

October 7, 2008
eSchool News

For the first time ever, technological literacy will become part of the National Assessment of Educational Progress (NAEP), also known as the Nation's Report Card, the test's governing board has announced.

Beginning in 2012, the test will measure students' proficiency with technology in addition to reading, math, science, history, writing, and other subjects. The new test will mark the first time students' technology literacy has been assessed on a national level.

The National Assessment Governing Board has awarded a $1.86 million contract to WestEd-a nonprofit educational research, development, and service agency based in San Francisco-to develop the 2012 NAEP Technological Literacy Framework. Under this new contract, awarded through a competitive bidding process, WestEd will recommend the framework and specifications for the 2012 NAEP Technological Literacy Assessment. Ultimately, WestEd's work will lead to ways to define and measure students' knowledge and skills in understanding important technological tools, the Governing Board said. Board members then will decide which grade level-fourth, eighth, or 12th-will be tested in 2012. "We are delighted to have WestEd help us lay the groundwork for an assessment in such an important area," said Darvin Winick, chairman of the Governing Board, which sets policy for NAEP. "Technology is changing and moving very fast, so accurate evaluation of student achievement in this area is essential." NAEP's Technological Literacy Assessment comes at a time when there are no nationwide requirements or common definitions for technological literacy.

The International Society for Technology in Education (ISTE) has developed a set of National Educational Technology Standards (NETS) for students, and the No Child Left Behind Act requires that students demonstrate technological literacy by the end of the eighth grade.

Yet only a handful of states have adopted separate tests in this area, even as a growing chorus of business representatives and policy makers voices concern about the ability of American students to compete in a global marketplace and keep up with quickly evolving technology. Several groups will help WestEd on this 18-month project, including ISTE, the Council of Chief State School Officers, the International Technology Education Association, the Partnership for 21st Century Skills, and the State Educational Technology Directors Association.

With this assistance, WestEd plans to convene two committees that will include technology experts, engineers, teachers, scientists, business representatives, state and local policy makers, and employers from across the country. The committees will advise WestEd on the content and design of the national tech literacy assessment. In addition, hundreds of experts in various fields-as well as the general public-will be able to participate in hearings or provide reviews of the framework document as it is developed. Ultimately, the collaboration will reflect the perspectives of a diverse array of individuals and groups, the Governing Board said. "WestEd has assembled a highly qualified team [composed] of exceptional organizations and knowledgeable individuals that bring a broad perspective on what students should know and be able to do in the area of technological literacy," said Steve Schneider, senior program director of WestEd's Mathematics, Science, and Technology Program. "We look forward to this opportunity to develop a framework that will guide the nation to a high-quality assessment of how our students meet the demands in this important international domain." The Governing Board is slated to review and approve the technological literacy framework in late 2009. "We all know that engineering and technologies in all forms-including computers, communications, energy usage, agriculture, medicine, and transportation-affect everything we hear, see, touch, and eat," said Alan J. Friedman, a physicist and member of the National Assessment Governing Board's Executive Committee. "With this new framework and the tests it will guide, we'll discover how well students today are learning to understand and use these immensely powerful tools."

Things to Think About

1. What do you think is important to include on technological literary assessment tests? Explain why.

2. How could assessment tests help improve effectiveness in teaching? Can you see any pitfalls in interpreting their results? Explain.

3. What about literacy in terms of social and ethical issues such as "sexting"? Where do they fit in terms of prioritizing the obligations of education and information literacy?

4. Many library faculty distinguish between information literacy and technological literacy. How would you explain the difference?

5. What about an international assessment test rather than a national one? What might be the advantages and disadvantages?

Key Terms

1. Technological literacy

2. National Assessment of Educational Progress

FORUM 17
Internet Safety

" An ounce of protection is worth a pound of cure," my mother often warned. The Broadband Data Improvement Act was passed in 2008 with just that in mind. The law requires the Federal Communications Commission (FCC) to carry out a national public awareness program that educates children on Internet safety.

At present, citizens may access a program, OnGuard Online, at http://www.onguardonline.gov. However, a quick perusal demonstrates that it is limited in content. For example, there are only three short videos now available. In addition, while there are numerous tutorials, there is no audio capability. It is hoped that the Broadband Data Improvement Act will greatly expand upon the programs now offered.

In addition, the law expands broadband data collection. For example, the Government Accountability Office will be required to compare U.S. broadband penetration with that of other countries. It will be required to create a study of the impact of broadband speeds on small businesses. It also requires reporting from wireless operators with subscribers that can browse the net with their phones and other devices; it will ask Voice-over-Internet-Protocol (VoIP) companies to report their customers, as well.

In learning about the law and its requirements, one can gain some understanding of how technology has changed. For example, for many years the commission had considered 200 Kbps to be "high speed"; it now considers the much faster 1.5 Mbps to be the top benchmark for "low speed." Essentially, the commission has redefined broadband (Condon, 2008).

Working with more accurate data that will provide information regarding demographics, we can determine just how much support is necessary for those who use technology. This may provide a better sense of the risks involved in using a particular technology, such as VoIP.

This data may also assist in providing for the health and safety of citizens indirectly. We can look closely upon certain geographic areas where there is concern in regard to the availability of Internet access, not just in terms of safety of the Web, but in securing the safety of the environment and the economy. In his keynote address to the Web 2.0 Summit in November 2008, former Vice President Al Gore, now a member of Apple's Board of Directors, stated, "Information is the dominant strategic resource of the economy in the 21st Century." He pointed out that access to information can help monitor the health of the planet. He also remarked that the iPhone and developments like it had transformed the political process, alluding to President Obama's use of his portable device for fundraising during the previous campaign (Krazil, 2008).

Although it is costly to report such data, the data can be processed to acquire powerful information. Protection must start with information—even information about information!

Article: Schools soon required to teach web safety

October 13, 2008
eSchool News

Schools receiving e-Rate discounts on their telecommunications services and internet access soon will have to educate their students about online safety, sexual predators, and cyber bullying, thanks to federal legislation passed in both the Senate and the House.

The Broadband Data Improvement Act (S.1492), sponsored by Senate Commerce Committee Chairman Daniel Inouye, D-Hawaii, requires the Federal Trade Commission to carry out a national public awareness program focused on educating children how to use the internet in safe and responsible ways. The legislation also establishes an "Online Safety and Technology Working Group" charged with evaluating online safety education efforts, parental control technologies, filtering and blocking software, and more.

As time ticked down on the 110th Congress, many people believed the original web-safety bill, the Protecting Children in the 21st Century Act, sponsored by Republican Sen. Ted Stevens of Alaska, would fail to see any final action. Stevens is on trial for allegedly failing to report gifts.

The Protecting Children in the 21st Century Act included language, supported by several educational technology advocacy groups, requiring schools receiving e-Rate funds to teach students about appropriate behavior on social networking and chat room web sites, as well as the dangers of cyber bullying.

The Senate Commerce Committee merged the language in Stevens' bill into the Broadband Data Improvement Act, which focuses on establishing new studies to track the penetration of U.S. broadband internet access. The bill passed through both chambers of Congress, and President Bush is expected to sign the legislation soon.

The bill reflects the concerns of parents, teachers, and others that children might meet sexual predators while on social networking sites or talking online in chat rooms. Increased media attention on online harassment and cyber bullying, including several cases where students have suffered severe emotional problems or have committed suicide after online taunts, also have influenced the bill.

Legislation introduced in 2006, the Deleting Online Predators Act, would have required schools and libraries to block access to social networking sites and chat rooms. But many K-12 groups opposed that bill, citing federal intrusion on school districts' rights to control content and arguing that education about safe and appropriate online behavior was a better approach.

Ed-tech advocacy groups are generally happy with the newly passed version of the legislation.

"The internet contains valuable content, collaboration, and communication opportunities that can, and do, materially contribute to a student's academic growth and preparation for the workforce," said representatives from the Consortium for School Networking and the International Society for Technology in Education in a joint statement.

"However, we recognize that students need to learn how to avoid inappropriate content and unwanted contacts from strangers while online. ... Educating students on how to keep themselves safe while online is the best line of defense, because no technological silver bullet has yet been devised that will guarantee that students are effectively protected. Therefore, we embrace wholeheartedly the thoughtful approach that S.1492 takes, particularly the flexibility that it affords districts on determining how best to educate students about staying safe online."

Inouye said passing the bill, which also will track the penetration of broadband service, is the first step to nationwide broadband access.

"If the United States is to remain a world leader in technology, we need a national broadband network that is second to none," he said. "The federal government has a responsibility to ensure the continued rollout of broadband access, as well as the successful deployment of the next generation of broadband technology."

Congress also approved a continuing resolution for FY09 appropriations that will fund all federal education programs—including the Enhancing Education Through Technology (EETT) block-grant program—at last year's levels until March 6. President Bush signed the appropriations measure on Sept. 30, the last day of the previous fiscal year.

The legislation means no final decision on FY09 education spending levels will be made until a new president takes office with a new Congress. Democrats are widely expected to retain control of Congress next year, though observers say the continuing financial crisis—coupled with wars in Iraq and Afghanistan—will make it exceedingly difficult for the nation's next president to push for additional education funds in FY09 and potentially FY10.

Things to Think About

1. What topics should be included in the content of the Enhancing Education Through Technology block-grant program? Would you include piracy and copyright infringement, for example?

2. List three types of Web sites in which Web safety is of paramount importance, especially for children.

3. Will teaching Web safety eliminate the need for school districts to control content? Is there still an ethical obligation to include filtering systems for children at school?

4. What technical obstacles are included in using filtering systems at schools? Is there a technical answer to overcoming them? What are your thoughts about the Deleting Online Predators Act?

5. Explain the new parameters for the "low end" of broadband speed. What are high end numbers? How significant is the change since the time the Internet became commercially available in 1984?

Key Terms

1. Deleting Online Predators Act

2. Protecting Children in the 21st Century Act

FORUM 18
Technology Research and Development

Have we taken the R out of R&D? Gary Anthes describes a trend that has moved from long term research to short term development. While billions are still spent on R&D according to corporate reports, "the pure research that led to the invention of the transistor and the Internet has steadily declined as companies bow to the pressure for quarterly and annual results." In addition, Anthes points out that academia vies for research funds but that University researchers spend much of their time developing proposals that never receive funding. We have certainly been there and done that!

Anthes further explains that agencies that formerly supplied funding for long-term research have recently focused on the short term needs of the functions of government, such as warfare and homeland security, "those who can promise measurable results in a year or two." In support of Anthes's arguments, the American Association for the Advancement of Science (AAAS) has presented evidence that "Federal research investments are shrinking as a share of the U.S. economy just as other nations are increasing their investments" (Koizumi, 2008).

What is the cost of limited pure research to the advancement of technology and the advancement of the economy?

Article: Dear Mr. President: Let's talk tech

By Gary Anthes
The New York Times
October 21, 2008

Science and technology may not have been the focus of the recent debates between presidential hopefuls John McCain and Barack Obama, but both candidates have outlined some broad policy proposals and goals. That's a good thing, because, as some of the top technology thinkers in the United States today recently shared with Computerworld, the next president will have to tackle the country's ongoing decline in global technological competitiveness.

Obama says he'll "change the posture of our federal government from being one of the most anti-science administrations in American history to one that embraces science and technology." He has promised to double federal funding of basic research over 10 years, to appoint the nation's first chief technology officer, to make the R&D tax credit for corporations permanent and to "restore the basic principle that government decisions should be based on the best-available, scientifically valid evidence and not on the ideological predispositions of agency officials or political appointees."

McCain has not said directly what he might do about the level of federal spending on research, but he has said he favors technology-friendly policies aimed at the private sector through "broad pools of capital, low taxes and incentives for research in America...and streamlining burdensome regulations." He says he'd make the R&D tax credit permanent and set it equal to 10% of the wages a company pays its R&D workers, and he says he'd allow companies to write off the cost of new technology and equipment in the first year.

Both candidates have outlined educational reforms that they say will make the U.S. more competitive in science and technology.

Computerworld recently asked nine high-tech luminaries to offer their advice to the next U.S. president. Their answers appear below. They represent the views of the individuals and not necessarily those of their employers.

Henry Chesbrough

Adjunct professor and executive director, Center for Open Innovation, Haas School of Business, University of California, Berkeley

The economic situation is as bad as it has been in decades. Innovation must be at the forefront of economic policies in [the new] administration. Innovation is widely distributed around the world, not concentrated in a few large firms in the U.S. alone. So policies must promote the division of innovation labor. These include support for start-ups and small businesses. Universities and national labs must be allowed to engage with industry on translating research results into commercial products. Markets for the sale and resale of intellectual property must be supported. Open initiatives must be promoted, especially where government can help set industry standards.

The environment for innovation must also be enhanced. More money must be appropriated for basic research. Ph.D. graduates should receive green cards to allow them to stay in the U.S. H1-B visas should be expanded. The R&D tax credit should be made permanent. And a new initiative in alternative energy led by the government—but involving universities, industry, venture capitalists, nonprofits and research labs—should be started immediately.

Judy Estrin

CEO, JLabs LLC; author of *Closing the Innovation Gap*

The future of our economy and our quality of life will depend on our ability to sustain a culture that supports and promotes the ability to innovate. The nation faces major challenges—energy independence and climate change, national security and the need for affordable, quality health care—that threaten our future. Each of these challenges also brings opportunities, if we give innovation the attention it deserves.

One of the most crucial roles of the next administration will be to foster the right environment for innovation through wise funding and smart policy. But it must also re-energize the nation by embracing these challenges, providing a vision to inspire and engage the country at large, and bring out the innovator in each of us.

Vinton Cerf

Internet pioneer; chief Internet evangelist, Google Inc.

We must take a global leadership role on energy and global warming. We should:

1. Focus our national R&D capacity on developing renewable energy at costs competitive with coal.

2. Continue work on clean coal and restart nuclear power development.

3. Begin a major campaign for reduction in fossil fuel consumption: 100 mpg hybrids and all-electric transportation.

4. Charge DARPA with development of new, lightweight, strong materials for automobile, air- and spacecraft bodies.

5. Initiate a crash program to analyze the effects of global warming on coastal regions, and prepare responses.

6. Increase funding for weather data collection, analysis and prediction to cope with effects of global warming

7. Develop a new K-12 educational program for science, technology, engineering and mathematics.

8. Make permanent the R&D tax credit, and initiate credit for use of renewable energy.

9. Strengthen the SEC and revisit banking regulations to prevent a repeat of the subprime mortgage and derivative security disaster.

10. Analyze and prepare for the massive wave of retiring baby boomers in the decade ahead.

David Farber

Professor of computer science, Carnegie Mellon University; former chief technologist, FCC

We have let the ability of the government to obtain advice and direction from leaders in IT decline over the past eight years. I propose that a new president re-establish the President's Information Technology Advisory Committee. This, combined with a strong science/technology adviser to the president, would provide the White House with much needed help in technology policy.

There are agencies that regulate aspects of IT, such as the Federal Communications Commission. Re-establishing the position of chief technologist as a permanent position [and establishing] a bureau that would attract technologists to join the agency would bring to the policymaking activities technical input and understanding missing these past years.

The Congress years ago lost the [Office of Technology Assessment, closed in 1995] that supplied it with studies and unbiased access to knowledge in IT. The establishment of an organization that has the staff and charter to advise the Congress can be critical in the formulation of realistic laws that impact IT. Such capability is missing now and our laws show it.

Finally, it is essential to get our brightest young scientists and technologists to intern in Washington. That requires a change in the attitudes of all levels of government and academia to recognize and reward these people for their services to the nation. The benefits to the nation and to the young future leaders who will be enormous and long-lasting.

Robert Kahn

Internet pioneer and former DARPA program manager; CEO of the Corporation for National Research Initiatives

I want [the new president] to focus on the critical importance of continued forward-looking investment and growth in science and technology. Innovations in science and technology allow us to compete effectively in the world, fueled by a university system of research and education that is still the envy of the world. National security and economic growth are closely coupled, and our engine of economic growth depends on an educated workforce and advances in technology.

Many of the greatest challenges we face in our cities, and with our globally interconnected world, are increasingly dependent on engineering talent that knows how to apply science and technology to solving real problems. In difficult times, when multiple near-term priorities draw heavily on limited resources, it is all too easy to curtail research investments and associated technology development. This would likely shortchange our future generations. The next president should firmly resist that possibility.

Leonard Kleinrock

Internet pioneer; professor of computer science, University of California, Los Angeles

The U.S. is facing serious challenges in maintaining its global leadership in many areas. When it comes to science and technology, we still enjoy a leadership position. But we are in serious danger of losing that position due to the shortsighted view of some of our key government funding agencies.

What used to be their willingness to support long-term, high-risk, high-payoff, well-funded and visionary research has been replaced with a focus on short-term, low-risk, low-payoff, poorly funded and pragmatic objectives. Not only is this damaging our ability to win in today's competitive environment, but also it is channeling the next generation of faculty and senior researchers into small science, incremental thinking and short-term goals. In other words, we are creating an impact on the current generation of researchers and are also damaging future generations of our research community. Our pipeline of producing excellent new scientists is diminishing due to this lack of proper funding.

I urge the next president to return to the generous government funding of long-term advanced and innovative research projects for our universities and research centers.

Ed Lazowska

Professor of computer science and engineering, University of Washington, Seattle; former chairman of the President's Information Technology Advisory Committee

1. Restore integrity to U.S. science policy. It is essential that federal policy benefit from the most complete, accurate and honest scientific and technological information available. The current administration has stacked scientific advisory boards, suppressed research that conflicts with its political agenda, prevented government scientists from speaking openly with the public and the media, failed to utilize the best available evidence to guide policy, and generally denigrated science, evidence and objectivity.

2. Double, over a 10-year period, the federal investment in fundamental research by key science agencies. Essentially every aspect of IT upon which we rely today traces its roots to federally sponsored research. The current administration has decreased federal support for fundamental research in all fields.

3. Make a national commitment to science education at all levels—K-12, undergraduate, graduate and retraining. Nothing is more important than the education of the next generation. America is losing ground.

4. Make the R&D tax credit permanent.

5. Use technology to address these "grand challenges" of the 21st century: achieving energy independence; addressing climate change; feeding the people of America and the world; enhancing national security; further improving human health, life expectancy and quality of life; restoring and improving our urban infrastructure; protecting our environment. Each is critical; none is optional. Each requires major new advances in science and technology.

Rick Rashid

Senior vice president, Microsoft Research; former professor of computer science, Carnegie Mellon University

Over the past 10 to 15 years, there has been a retreat from the successful research investment strategies of the past—strategies that created modern computing and the Internet. Increasing use of noncompetitive earmarked funding, short-term mission focused investment and insufficient funding for long-term and risk-taking research threaten America's economic future and position in the world.

My advice to a new administration is to work toward restoring a balanced system of support for long-term basic research in science and technology with a goal of ensuring the future competitiveness of the U.S.

Specifically, I would recommend to a new administration that it work with Congress to eliminate or limit earmark funding for science, restore the "long-term risk-taking" parts of DARPA to its 1970s/1980s form, and fund the American Competitiveness Initiative.

Victor Zue

Director of the MIT Computer Science and Artificial Intelligence Laboratory; adviser to the U.S. Department of Defense and National Science Foundation

Advances in information technology and computer science (IT&CS) have fundamentally changed the way we live, work, learn and play, and have driven progress in many fields like weather prediction and computational genomics. More important, they are the primary force that powers our economy.

At a time of worldwide economic, geopolitical and social challenges, the next president must ensure our continuing preeminence in IT&CS. Historically, revolutionary achievements—the Internet, mobile communication, parallel computing, graphical user interfaces—typically originated from university research and often took more than a decade to realize a $1 billion market.

Therefore, the administration must significantly increase its budget for long-term, fundamental research, e.g., by doubling the NSF budget annually for the next four years. We must invest in educating the next generation of IT&CS professionals. This will require introducing courses in high school and ensuring that those who would like to enter the field can afford it.

Things to Think About

1. Of the nine experts, whose advice would you suggest to the president as a top priority? Explain.

2. President Obama is the first U.S. president to use a BlackBerry. What are the implications for his productivity?

3. What are the concerns of the AAAS? What are your recommendations for funding research?

4. What are the tax benefits for corporations for research and development? Could changes in tax laws significantly entice industry to provide more R&D dollars?

5. What are the technology friendly policies that McCain favored? Do you agree with them?

Key Terms

1. Technology friendly policies

2. Research and development tax credit

FORUM 19
Cybercrime Investigations: Botnets and Honeypots

Conficker was breaking news as Microsoft put out a bounty of a quarter of a million dollars to catch those responsible for the self-replicating worm that takes advantage of those who have not updated their Windows software with available patches. It is recorded as one of the worst malware attacks in the last 5 years, attacking about 9 million computers within 5 days.

Hospitals across Sheffield, United Kingdom, were attacked when information system managers turned off security patches after a computer rebooted in an operating room during surgery, leaving 8,000 computers vulnerable to the attack. It is believed 800 computers carried the worm, causing the cancellation of appointments for nonemergency care for patients.

It is particularly dangerous because it hides on USB memory sticks (flash drives) and amasses "zombie machines into botnet armies" (Yahoo Tech, 2009). Most troubling, however, is that it used botnets to crack passwords using what is termed a "brute force" approach (Arthur, 2009). Therefore, security specialists recommend strengthening or "hardening" passwords by mixing in numbers, punctuation marks, and uppercase letters. After cracking the code, the worm tries to connect to up to 250 domains. When computers connect to any one of these domains, they become infected.

Article: A Robot Network Seeks to Enlist Your Computer

By John Markoff
October 20, 2008
The New York Times

REDMOND, Wash.— In a windowless room on Microsoft's campus here, T. J. Campana, a cybercrime investigator, connects an unprotected computer running an early version of Windows XP to the Internet. In about 30 seconds the computer is "owned."

An automated program lurking on the Internet has remotely taken over the PC and turned it into a "zombie." That computer and other zombie machines are then assembled into systems called "botnets"—home and business PCs that are hooked together into a vast chain of cyber-robots that do the bidding of automated programs to send the majority of e-mail spam, to illegally seek financial information and to install malicious software on still more PCs.

Botnets remain an Internet scourge. Active zombie networks created by a growing criminal underground peaked last month at more than half a million computers, according to shadowserver.org, an organization that tracks botnets. Even though security experts have diminished the botnets to about 300,000 computers, that is still twice the number detected a year ago.

The actual numbers may be far larger; Microsoft investigators, who say they are tracking about 1,000 botnets at any given time, say the largest network still controls several million PCs.

"The mean time to infection is less than five minutes," said Richie Lai, who is part of Microsoft's Internet Safety Enforcement Team, a group of about 20 researchers and investigators. The team is tackling a menace that in the last five years has grown from a computer hacker pastime to a dark business that is threatening the commercial viability of the Internet.

Any computer connected to the Internet can be vulnerable. Computer security executives recommend that PC owners run a variety of commercial malware detection programs, like Microsoft's Malicious Software Removal Tool, to find infections of their computers. They should also protect the PCs behind a firewall and install security patches for operating systems and applications.

Even these steps are not a sure thing. Last week Secunia, a computer security firm, said it had tested a dozen leading PC security suites and found that the best one detected only 64 out of 300 software vulnerabilities that make it possible to install malware on a computer.

Botnet attacks now come with their own antivirus software, permitting the programs to take over a computer and then effectively remove other malware competitors. Mr. Campana said the Microsoft investigators were amazed recently to find a botnet that turned on the Microsoft Windows Update feature after taking over a computer, to defend its host from an invasion of competing infections.

Botnets have evolved quickly to make detection more difficult. During the last year botnets began using a technique called fast-flux, which involved generating a rapidly changing set of Internet addresses to make the botnet more difficult to locate and disrupt.

Companies have realized that the only way to combat the menace of botnets and modern computer crime is to build a global alliance that crosses corporate and national boundaries. On Tuesday, Microsoft, the world's largest software company, will convene a gathering of the International Botnet Taskforce in Arlington, Va. At the conference, which is held twice a year, more than 175 members of government and law enforcement agencies, computer security companies and academics will discuss the latest strategies, including legal efforts.

Although the Microsoft team has filed more than 300 civil lawsuits against botnet operators, the company also relies on enforcement agencies like the F.B.I. and Interpol-related organizations for criminal prosecution.

Last month the alliance received support from new federal legislation, which for the first time specifically criminalized the use of botnets. Many of the bots are based in other countries, however, and Mr. Campana said there were many nations with no similar laws.

"It's really a sort of cat-and-mouse situation with the underground," said David Dittrich, a senior security engineer at the University of Washington Applied Physics Laboratory and a member of the International Botnet Taskforce. "Now there's profit motive, and the people doing stuff for profit are doing unique and interesting things."

Microsoft's botnet hunters, who have kept a low profile until now, are led by Richard Boscovich, who until six months ago served as a federal prosecutor in Miami. Mr. Boscovich, a federal prosecutor for 18 years, said he was optimistic that despite the growing number of botnets, progress was being made against computer crime. Recent successes have led to arrests.

"Every time we have a story that says bot-herders get locked up, that helps," said Mr. Boscovich, who in 2000 helped convict Jonathan James, a teenage computer hacker who had gained access to Defense Department and National Air and Space Administration computers.

To aid in its investigations, the Microsoft team has built elaborate software tools including traps called "honeypots" that are used to detect malware and a system called the Botnet Monitoring and Analysis Tool. The software is installed in several refrigerated server rooms on the Microsoft campus that are directly connected to the open Internet, both to mask its location and to make it possible to deploy software sensors around the globe.

The door to the room simply reads "the lab." Inside are racks of hundreds of processors and terabytes of disk drives needed to capture the digital evidence that must be logged as carefully as evidence is maintained by crime scene investigators.

Detecting and disrupting botnets is a particularly delicate challenge that Microsoft will talk about only in vague terms. Their challenge parallels the traditional one of law enforcement's placing informers inside criminal gangs.

Just as gangs will often force a recruit to commit a crime as a test of loyalty, in cyberspace, bot-herders will test recruits in an effort to weed out spies. Microsoft investigators would not discuss their solution to this problem, but said they avoided doing anything illegal with their software.

One possible approach would be to create sensors that would fool the bot-herders by appearing to do malicious things, but in fact not perform the actions.

In 2003 and 2004 Microsoft was deeply shaken by a succession of malicious software worm programs with names like "Blaster" and "Sasser," that raced through the Internet, sowing chaos within corporations and among home computer users. Blaster was a personal affront to the software firm that has long prided itself on its technology prowess.

The program contained a hidden message mocking Microsoft's co-founder: "billy gates why do you make this possible? Stop making money and fix your software!!"

The company maintains that its current software is less vulnerable, but even as it fixed some problems, the threat to the world's computers has become far greater. Mr. Campana said that there had been ups and downs in the fight against a new kind of criminal who could hide virtually anywhere in the world and strike with devilish cleverness.

"I come in every morning, and I think we're making progress," he said. At the same time, he said, botnets are not going to go away any time soon.

"There are a lot of very smart people doing very bad things," he said.

Things to Think About

1. How are botnets tracked? Visit http://shadowserver.org.

2. What new programs exist to protect Windows operating systems such as Vista?

3. What recent malicious software worms have arisen? What new strategy has industry implemented to deal with them?

4. How is Microsoft going on the offensive against botnets? What pragmatic steps can users employ to avoid the dangers of botnets and zombies?

5. What is the danger of using USB memory sticks? Why did the U.S. Department of Defense ban their use?

Key Terms

1. Security patch

2. Zombie

FORUM 20
Global Network Governance

The Internet may be deemed as a world of its own, but in fact, online organizations are often forced to adhere to local laws. There are products and services that will not be accessible to consumers from electronic commercial enterprises if the local laws do not permit their sale.

The Australian Surveillance Devices Act, for example, requires that private investigators must obtain the consent of their targets in order to track them (Riddle, 2009).

The Internet Commerce Association monitors legal matters for online businesses and is concerned about the inability of industry to adhere to the local laws established throughout the world. What is the future of ecommerce?

Article: Online Businesses Subject to Local Laws Everywhere

By Ben Worthen
The Wall Street Journal
October 21, 2008

A judge in Kentucky seized the Web addresses of more than 140 Internet-gambling sites last week, the latest example of how local governments can affect online businesses with physical operations beyond their jurisdictions.

It is common to think of the Internet as a global network that transcends geography. But online entities are often forced to adhere to laws in the places where they do business. One iconic example is a ruling by a French court in 2000, where the court said a French law banning the sale of Nazi paraphernalia applied to U.S.-based Web site Yahoo.

In the Kentucky case, Circuit Court Judge Thomas Wingate concluded that gambling Web sites were "virtual keys" that provided access to places where one could play online versions of gambling devices such as slot machines and roulette tables, which are illegal in the state.

None of the online businesses—such as GoldenPalace.com, PokerStars.com and UltimateBet.com—are based in Kentucky or rely on technical equipment located in the state. Still, the sites readily accept bets placed by users in Kentucky and process payments from banks based there. That is what triggered Judge Wingate to seize control of the Web addresses.

"Seizing," it should be noted, sounds more ominous than it is when applied to the Internet realm. It prevents an Internet registrar that issues Web site names from transferring a Web address to a different registrar, even if the owner of the address, such as a gambling site, requests it. The gambling sites will remain operational until the judge issues a forfeiture order, at which point they will become state property.

The court said it will lift its seizure order for online casinos if they implement technology that would block Kentucky residents from accessing their sites.

Groups affiliated with the online casinos are worried about the precedent the ruling sets. "If you're a business operator, you should be subject to the laws where you do and pursue business, and not have to worry about a state halfway around the world taking away your storefront," says Jeremiah Johnston, president of the Internet Commerce Association, which monitors legal matters for online businesses. He adds that there is no reason that other governments couldn't use the same technique to challenge online businesses for whatever reason they choose.

Todd Greene, an attorney for Oversee.net, which has a subsidiary called Moniker Online Services that is the registrar for two of the gambling sites, says he doesn't believe that the Kentucky court has the jurisdiction to order the seizure. While Moniker has frozen the domain names for now—effectively following the court order—it is doing so as a matter of policy.

J. Michael Brown, secretary of justice and public safety for Kentucky, who brought the lawsuit, says he only wants to stop what he considers an illegal activity.

A final hearing is set for November.

Update: We want to make it clear that the Web sites and registrars aren't just sitting by, but intend to challenge both the Kentucky courts ruling and its jurisdiction in the matter.

Things to Think About

1. Can you think of businesses other than online gambling to which local governance issues would apply?

2. What differences exist in privacy regulations among different industrialized nations?

3. What is the argument made by the Internet Commerce Association? Is it valid?

4. How would you argue in defense of a nation that supports governance of local laws?

5. What implications will this have for conducting online business? How does seizing work?

Key Terms

1. Internet Commerce Association

2. Seizing

FORUM 21
Digital Politics and Copyright Law

The Digital Millennium Copyright Act, otherwise known as the DMCA, was at the heart of a debate between the John McCain U.S. presidential campaign and YouTube.com.

YouTube removed McCain commercials because they included televised news broadcasts in which permission from the news agencies had never been granted.

McCain voted for the DMCA, as a United States senator, which includes a provision for fair use. It was the McCain campaign's position that their video commercial is covered under the fair use provision of the DMCA.

Fair use is a legal doctrine that allows the public to make limited uses of copyrighted works without permission. Fair use depends on the balancing of four factors: (1) the purpose of the use, (2) the nature of the work, (3) the amount of the work used, and (4) the effect of the use on the market for the original work (http://www.umuc.edu/library/copy.shtml).

Determination of what is "fair use" is clearly not a simple matter.

Article: McCain Fights for the Right to Remix on YouTube

By Saul Hansell
October 14, 2008
The New York Times
(UPDATED 10/15: Added YouTube's response)

Internet issues have taken a back seat in the presidential campaign. But this week, even as Senator John McCain unveiled his new economic plan, he also introduced a new position on copyright law.

Trevor Potter, the general counsel for the McCain-Palin presidential campaign, sent a letter on Monday to Chad Hurley, the chief executive of YouTube, complaining that the video service, now owned by Google, had inappropriately removed McCain commercials from its site.

The commercials incorporated snippets of television news broadcasts. Using provisions of the Digital Millennium Copyright Act, the news organizations demanded that the commercials be removed from YouTube because they violated the organizations' copyrights.

Mr. Potter praised YouTube as a "platform for political candidates and the American public to post, view, share, discuss, comment on, mash up, remix and argue over campaign-related videos." Then he argued that the excerpts of news broadcasts represented a fair use, which exempted them from control by the copyright owner:

The uses at issue have been the inclusion of fewer than 10 seconds of footage from news broadcasts in campaign ads or videos, as a basis for commentary on the issues presented in the news reports.

In one case, a McCain commercial included a clip of the CBS anchor Katie Couric talking about sexism in coverage of Senator Hillary Clinton. CBS argued that the use of the clip implied that it was endorsing the McCain campaign.

The letter from the McCain camp didn't mention it, but the campaign itself has run into copyright claims from the music industry, as Wired noted today:

One of its highest profile hits on the web, "Obama Love," for example, faced an embarrassing revamp in July when YouTube received a D.M.C.A. take-down notice from The Warner Music Group. The campaign had used Franki Valli's hit tune "Can't Take My Eyes Off Of You" as the video's sarcastic soundtrack.

Like many others whose work has been removed from Internet sites because of the copyright act, Mr. Potter complained about how the act's provisions seem to favor copyright owners. If the creator of a video complains that it has been removed inappropriately, the act does not allow it to be put back on the Internet for 10 to 14 days. He wrote:

But 10 days can be a lifetime in a political campaign, and there is no justification for depriving the American people of access to important and timely campaign videos during that period.

Mr. Potter proposed that YouTube itself review all demands asking that videos from politicians be removed, to determine if the copyrighted material was covered by the fair use exemption. Most Internet sites want to avoid becoming judges in such legal disputes.

UPDATED:

I've asked YouTube for comment and will post its response if it gets back to me. In a letter back to the McCain campaign late Tuesday, YouTube said that while abuses of the D.M.C.A. takedown process occur, it's difficult for the company to know who owns the rights to various elements of videos, even a campaign video.

Furthermore, YouTube said that while presidential campaign content was important, "there is a lot of other content on our global site that our users around the world find to be equally important." YouTube continued:

We try to be careful not to favor one category of content on our site over others, and to treat all of our users fairly, regardless of whether they are an individual, a large corporation or a candidate for public office....

On a final note, we hope that as a content uploader, you have gained a sense of some of the challenges we face everyday in operating YouTube. We look forward to working with Senator (or President) McCain on ways to combat abuse of the D.M.C.A. takedown process on YouTube, including, by way of example, strengthening the fair use doctrine....

Until now, Senator McCain has not had much common cause with the Internet free speech movement. He voted for the D.M.C.A., and he opposes legislation to enforce network neutrality. So not surprisingly, the advocacy groups jumped to highlight the irony of the campaign's letter.

Gigi Sohn, the president of the digital rights group Public Knowledge, used the incident to argue that copyright law gives too much power to the copyright holders:

The Digital Millennium Copyright Act (D.M.C.A.) was originally designed by, and for, the big media companies. The concepts of fair use then, as now, are largely ignored or shuffled off to the side when any Congressional discussion of copyright law takes place. The D.M.C.A. passed in 1998 without a hint of opposition in the House and in the Senate. YouTube was abiding by the rules that Congress set up when it took down the videos about which the McCain/Palin campaign complained.

And Fred von Lohmann, a lawyer for the Electronic Frontier Foundation, challenged the campaign's proposed solution:

It assumes that YouTube should prioritize the campaigns' fair use rights, rather than those of the rest of us. That seems precisely backwards, since the most exciting new possibilities on YouTube are for amateur political expression by the voters themselves. After all, the campaigns have no trouble getting the same ads out on television and radio, options not available to most YouTubers.

If the polls are to be believed, we may never know what how much a McCain administration would fight for everyone's right to make mash-ups.

Things to Think About

1. Do you think that the remixing of YouTube videos impacts the support of voters?

2. How did the DMCA enter into the argument against McCain's videos? What was the argument by his campaign?

3. How does this case impact the future use of videos in campaigns? Were there any preliminary actions that might have avoided this problem?

4. Explain fair use. How does it impact your research?

5. Do you see the existing laws under fair use as fair to consumers? Explain.

Key Terms

1. Remix

2. DMCA

FORUM 22
Digital Authentication: Cryptography

Should the ability to develop an effective password be on technological literacy exams? Cryptography is the practice and study of hiding information. Almost 15 years after the Internet became commercially available, most consumers still choose passwords that are short and fairly easy to detect.

Such was the case of the University of Tennessee student determining with ease the password chosen by Sarah Palin for her personal email account. Simply using the information he learned from the media, he could answer correctly the questions asked in order to reset her password (Lakin, 2008).

Coincidentally, it is reported that the same held true for the student. Knowing that his last name was Kernel, the FBI conjectured that "popcorn" might be a password he would have chosen. Bingo!

Does this problem signal that it is time to rely on the hardware to determine the password?

Article: Goodbye, Passwords. You Aren't a Good Defense.

By Randall Stross
August 10, 2008
The New York Times

The best password is a long, nonsensical string of letters and numbers and punctuation marks, a combination never put together before. Some admirable people actually do memorize random strings of characters for their passwords—and replace them with other random strings every couple of months.

Then there's the rest of us, selecting the short, the familiar and the easiest to remember. And holding onto it forever.

I once felt ashamed about failing to follow best practices for password selection—but no more. Computer security experts say that choosing hard-to-guess passwords ultimately brings little security protection. Passwords won't keep us safe from identity theft, no matter how clever we are in choosing them.

That would be the case even if we had done a better job of listening to instructions. Surveys show that we've remained stubbornly fond of perennial favorites like "password," "123456" and "LetMeIn." The underlying problem, however, isn't their simplicity. It's the log-on procedure itself, in which we land on a Web page, which may or may not be what it says it is, and type in a string of characters to authenticate our identity (or have our password manager insert the expected string on our behalf).

This procedure—which now seems perfectly natural because we've been trained to repeat it so much—is a bad idea, one that no security expert whom I reached would defend.

Password-based log-ons are susceptible to being compromised in any number of ways. Consider a single threat, that posed by phishers who trick us into clicking to a site designed to mimic a legitimate one in order to harvest our log-on information. Once we've been suckered at one site and our password purloined, it can be tried at other sites.

The solution urged by the experts is to abandon passwords—and to move to a fundamentally different model, one in which humans play little or no part in logging on. Instead, machines have a cryptographically encoded conversation to establish both parties' authenticity, using digital keys that we, as users, have no need to see.

In short, we need a log-on system that relies on cryptography, not mnemonics.

As users, we would replace passwords with so-called information cards, icons on our screen that we select with a click to log on to a Web site. The click starts a handshake between machines that relies on hard-to-crack cryptographic code. The necessary software for creating information cards is on only about 20 percent of PCs, though that's up from 10 percent a year ago. Windows Vista machines are equipped by default, but Windows XP, Mac and Linux machines require downloads.

And that's only half the battle: Web site hosts must also be persuaded to adopt information-card technology for sign-ons.

We won't make much progress on information cards in the near future, however, because of wasted energy and attention devoted to a large distraction, the OpenID initiative. OpenID promotes "Single Sign-On": with it, logging on to one OpenID Web site with one password will grant entrance during that session to all Web sites that accept OpenID credentials.

OpenID offers, at best, a little convenience, and ignores the security vulnerability inherent in the process of typing a password into someone else's Web site. Nevertheless, every few months another brand-name company announces that it has become the newest OpenID signatory. Representatives of Google, I.B.M., Microsoft and Yahoo are on OpenID's guiding board of corporations. Last month, when MySpace announced that it would support the standard, the nonprofit foundation.

OpenID.net boasted that the number of "OpenID enabled users" had passed 500 million and that "it's clear the momentum is only just starting to pick up."

Support for OpenID is conspicuously limited, however. Each of the big powers supposedly backing OpenID is glad to create an OpenID identity for visitors, which can be used at its site, but it isn't willing to rely upon the OpenID credentials issued by others. You can't use Microsoft-issued OpenID at Yahoo, nor Yahoo's at Microsoft.

Why not? Because the companies see the many ways that the password-based log-on process, handled elsewhere, could be compromised. They do not want to take on the liability for mischief originating at someone else's site.

When I asked Scott Kveton, chairman of the OpenID Foundation's community board, about criticism of OpenID, he said candidly, "Passwords, we know, are totally broken." He said new security options, such as software that works with OpenID that installs within the browser, are being offered. When it comes to security, he said, "there is no silver bullet, and there never will be."

Kim Cameron, Microsoft's chief architect of identity, is an enthusiastic advocate of information cards, which are not only vastly more secure than a password-based security system, but are also customizable, permitting users to limit what information is released to particular sites. "I don't like Single Sign-On," Mr. Cameron said. "I don't believe in Single Sign-On."

Microsoft and Google are among the six founding companies of the Information Card Foundation, formed to promote adoption of the card technology. The presence of PayPal, which is owned by eBay, in the group is the most significant: PayPal, with its direct access to our checking accounts, will naturally be inclined to be conservative. If it becomes convinced that these cards are more secure than passwords, we should listen.

BUT perhaps information cards in certain situations are convenient to a fault, permitting anyone who happens by a PC that is momentarily unattended in an office setting to click quickly through a sign-on at a Web site holding sensitive information. This need not pose a problem, however.

"Users on shared systems can easily set up a simple PIN code to protect any card from use by other users," Mr. Cameron said.

The PIN doesn't return us to the Web password mess: it never leaves our machine and can't be seen by phishers.

Unlearning the habit of typing a password into a box on a Web page will take a long while, but it's needed for our own protection. Logging on to a site should entail a cryptographic conversation between machines, saving us from inadvertently giving away the keys.

No more relying on our old companion "LetMeIn."

Things to Think About

1. How does the use of a password create vulnerabilities in security? What are the rules for the development of strong passwords? Provide examples. Why do users resist the development of strong passwords?

2. Explain how cryptography could be described as hardware driven rather than software driven. Explain how the use of cryptography might appear to follow a trend already adopted by Web 2.0 in using remote servers to control our database and software needs?

3. How does cryptography provide a solution for password vulnerabilities in relation to phishing?

4. Compare cryptography and mnemonics. How viable is it for most organizations to move to this system? Assuming you were delivering IS solutions to your firm, what would be the platform necessary to implement cryptography? What are the present obstacles and how could they be overcome? Explain.

5. How might the use of OpenID benefit an organization? What are the risks? What could you point to that suggests that many firms administering OpenID are aware of vulnerabilities? Go to the Ebay and PayPal Web sites. How does PayPal take the lead in the information card foundation?

Key Terms

1. Cryptography

2. Mnemonics

FORUM 23
The Power of Information

Doubt, is the name of a recent movie nominated for five Academy Awards. In the movie, a priest provides a lesson to his congregation on the power of words and the difficulty in making amends to those whose reputations have been scarred:

A group of ladies got together for tea. As they sipped their sassafras, they talked about the neighborhood, and shared their "concerns" about its inhabitants.

Later, one of the ladies realized that she might be guilty of gossip. So, the next day when she went to confession, she asked the priest if what she had done would be considered gossip. And, if so, should she confess it? The priest assured her that it was in fact gossip. Instead of the traditional "Hail Mary's" and "Our Father's," he told her to go home and find her favorite sleeping pillow. Then, go to the kitchen, grab the butcher knife, and proceed to the roof of the building...stab the pillow until if was ripped apart. She was instructed to leave it there and return to confession the next day. As instructed, the next day she returned to the confessional. "Did you follow my instructions?" She had. "What happened to the pillow?" "Well," she said, "it made a horrible mess. There were feathers blowing all over the neighborhood. It looked like it was snowing!" "Now, I'd like you to go back to your neighborhood and pick up all of the feathers," the priest instructed. The woman was horrified. "I can't do that! They have spread throughout the neighborhood. I could never find all of them!" "Exactly," said the priest. "And so it is with gossip" (Pastor Bob's Blog, 2008).

How would you feel if outdated or false information about you was provided to an employer?

Recently, a breech of confidence seriously impacted a corporate institution, United Airlines. An article appeared that indicated that the airlines had just filed for bankruptcy. What someone missed was the date on the article. When picked up by Google News and viewed by stockholders, the stock plunged! Now, all involved are attempting to determine to quantify the damages and identify those responsible.

Historically, marketers have believed that there is no such thing as negative publicity. The idea focused on the power of name recognition. One wonders now if instant availability of information may have permanently changed that premise. Retrieval of information attached to the identity of an organization or a person is so easily achieved that it may now impact reputation in a much more profound way.

What is the economic loss to United? Are we as concerned about the economic loss to individuals as we are about the loss to industry?

Article: Probe into how Google mix-up caused $1 billion run on United

By Mike Harvey
September 12, 2008
Times Online

The US Securities and Exchange Commission has opened a "preliminary inquiry" into how an outdated bankruptcy story sparked a $1 billion run on an airline's stock value.

The article about how United Airlines filed for bankruptcy in 2002 was revived when it showed up on a newspaper site's "most viewed" section on Monday.

From there it was picked up by Google News and later seen by alarmed stockholders. The stock plunged from around $12 to just $3 a share before trading was halted.

The Chicago-based company's shares did not fully recover once trading resumed on Monday, and were still down at just over $11 dollars at close of trading yesterday.

With the possiblity of legal action in the air, those involved have been hotly disputing who was to blame.

The errors provide a salutary lesson for investors of the power and perils of computer automation and throw a spotlight on Google's News search technology which, using "Googlebot" algorithms, scours web pages in search of news articles.

To many, the episode has been a reminder that computer programs, no matter how sophisticated, can be a poor substitute for human beings.

The comedy of errors began with just one reader who went to the South Florida Sun Sentinel's website and viewed a 2002 article on United Airlines' bankruptcy.

That single visit in the early hours of Sunday morning, a period of low traffic, apparently bumped it into a "Popular Stories" in the business section.

At 1:37am, an electronic Google program swept through the paper's website for new stories and spotted the link.

Google says its program scanned the piece and, seeing there was no 2002 dateline, indexed the article for inclusion on its news pages.

Three minutes and two seconds later, Google News readers started viewing the story on the Sun Sentinel's Web site.

A Florida investment firm found the story on Monday morning with a Google search and posted a summary on the Bloomberg financial information service.

That visibility—Bloomberg is seen by thousands of investment managers and traders—sparked the run on United shares.

What is in dispute between Tribune, the owners of the Sun Sentinel, and Google is whether the Googlebot should have known it was an old story.

Tribune said the story was not republished, and the link was simply a link to the archive version of the story.

Google spokesman Gabriel Stricker said that the only date the automated Google News software found on the Sun Sentinel site was from early Sunday eastern time.

"In the same way that the reader was unable to determine the original date, our search algorithm was similarly misled by that date," Mr Stricker said.

Tribune spokesman Gary Weitman said other clues would have made it clear to a human reader that the story was old, including a reference to UAL's 97-cent share price (it was trading around $12 on Monday) and comments from readers further down the page that were posted in 2002.

"It appears that no one who passed this story along actually bothered to read the story itself," he said.

"Despite the company's earlier request and the confusion caused by Googlebot and Google News earlier this week, we believe that Googlebot continues to misclassify stories," Tribune said.

The investment newsletter that posted a summary of the story to Bloomberg, Income Securities Advisors Inc. in Florida, has also said there was nothing on the Sun Sentinel website to indicate that the story was old.

The page also fooled Bloomberg. Bloomberg News staffers posted headlines noting first the UAL share price drop, and then, at 11:06 a.m. EDT, a bankruptcy denial from United.

A different Bloomberg News staffer working the story found the bankruptcy story on the Sun Sentinel site and, at 11:07a.m., posted a headline about the bankruptcy.

Investors then dumped the stock at a huge rate and here algorithms again played their part.

Experts said the automated trading programs were applied to the trading of shares based on market-moving information trawled from the internet.

Last year, algorithms handled some 30 percent of all equity trading volume, according to a recent study by Aite Group.

The study projected that algorithms would grow to handle half of equity trading by 2010, and noted similar growth in derivatives and other asset classes as a hunger for faster trading grows.

The lack of confidence investors have in the troubled US airline industry also undoubtedly played its part in the stock drop.

Investors mistakenly figured that United Airlines, having filed for bankruptcy once, was more likely to do it again.

United is still considering what, if anything, to do about the affair.

Things to Think About

1. Is it the responsibility of the consumer to view information on the Web critically? If the date on the article was correct, is the agency who posted it liable?

2. What were the damages to United? Who will make this determination? Is there sufficient action that could be taken to mitigate the damages?

3. How do you think the article ended up in "Popular Stories"?

4. Should a different set of standards be held for personal violations of false news reports than ones that affect industry? What are the costs of personal violations?

5. Do the risks associated with this program outweigh its cost benefit?

Key Terms

1. Googlebot Algorithms

2. Securities and Exchange Commission

FORUM 24
Deep-Packet Inspection

C an you remember when the word "cookie" invoked the most satisfying of all human sensations, especially the chocolate chip ones that were just removed from the oven? Well, if you have come to the conclusion that a "cookie" will never be the same, think again. That is because electronic cookies and the "crumbs" they leave behind may no longer exist at the forefront of your data monitoring concerns for the future. Do you remember your techie friends who so cautiously deleted their cookies in a timely manner, in order to outsmart the marketers who sought to learn just how many times they had visited their websites? Or maybe you know someone who wanted to be sure his girlfriend had no way of knowing he had visited her rival's Facebook page?

Cookies do still serve a function for most organizations. You will note that those who allow your access to secured databases, such as those who manage private course management sites, will still require that you enable cookies before you are able to successfully enter the site. This acts as a security measure for documenting an audit trail if a violation in the use of the secured database should take place by the user.

In fact, cookie programs may be considered obsolete for the purpose of monitoring customer needs and purchasing decisions. You may be surprised to learn that the tactics used to secure your "private" clicks have now been outmaneuvered once again. This time, however, much more significant data is collected – data which may reveal much about your life experiences. In simplistic terms, just as the name implies, data sent over the Internet is organized into packets for speedy transmission. Who needs cookies when a monitoring service will be happy to inspect your "data packets" for information about you that Internet Service Providers (ISP) plan to sell to marketers?

Data denial is no longer an option.

Article: Every Click You Make: Internet Providers Quietly Test Expanded Tracking of Web Use to Target Advertising

By Peter Whoriskey
The Washington Post
Friday, April 4, 2008

The online behavior of a small but growing number of computer users in the United States is monitored by their Internet service providers, who have access to every click and keystroke that comes down the line.

The companies harvest the stream of data for clues to a person's interests, making money from advertisers who use the information to target their online pitches.

The practice represents a significant expansion in the ability to track a household's Web use because it taps into Internet connections, and critics liken it to a phone company listening in on conversations. But the companies involved say customers' privacy is protected because no personally identifying details are released.

The extent of the practice is difficult to gauge because some service providers involved have declined to discuss their practices. Many Web surfers, moreover, probably have little idea they are being monitored.

But at least 100,000 U.S. customers are tracked this way, and service providers have been testing it with as many as 10 percent of U.S. customers, according to tech companies involved in the data collection.

Although common tracking systems, known as cookies, have counted a consumer's visits to a network of sites, the new monitoring, known as "deep-packet inspection," enables a far wider view—every Web page visited, every e-mail sent and every search entered. Every bit of data is divided into packets—like electronic envelopes—that the system can access and analyze for content.

"You don't want the phone company tapping your phone calls, and in the same way you don't want your ISP tapping your Web traffic," said Ari Schwartz of the Center for Democracy and Technology, an advocacy group. "There's a fear here that a user's ISP is going to betray them and turn their information over to a third party."

In fact, newly proposed Federal Trade Commission guidelines for behavioral advertising have been outpaced by the technology and do not address the practice directly. Privacy advocates are preparing to present to Congress their concerns that the practice is done without consumer consent and that too little is known about whether such systems adequately protect personal information.

Meanwhile, many online publishers say the next big growth in advertising will emerge from efforts to offer ads based not on the content of a Web page, but on knowing who is looking at it. That, of course, means gathering more information about consumers.

Advocates of deep-packet inspection see it as a boon for all involved. Advertisers can better target their pitches. Consumers will see more relevant ads. Service providers who hand over consumer data can share in advertising revenues. And Web sites can make more money from online advertising, a $20 billion industry that is growing rapidly.

With the service provider involved in collecting consumer data, "there is access to a broader spectrum of the Web traffic—it's significantly more valuable," said Derek Maxson, chief technology officer of Front Porch, a company that collects such data from millions of users in Asia and is working with a number of U.S. service providers.

Consider, say, the Boston Celtics Web site. Based on its content, it posts ads for products a Celtics fan might be interested in: Adidas, a Boston hotel and so on.

With information about users from deep-packet inspection, however, advertisers might learn that the person looking at the Celtics Web site is also a potential car customer because he recently visited the Ford site and searched in Google for "best minivans." That means car companies might be interested in sending an ad to that user at the Celtics site, too.

For all its promise, however, the service providers exploring and testing such services have largely kept quiet—"for fear of customer revolt," according to one executive involved.

It is only through the companies that design the data collection systems—companies such as NebuAd, Phorm and Front Porch—that it is possible to gauge the technology's spread. Front Porch collects detailed Web-use data from more than 100,000 U.S. customers through their service providers, Maxson said. NebuAd has agreements with providers covering 10 percent of U.S. broadband customers, chief executive Bob Dykes said.

In England, Phorm is expected in the coming weeks to launch its monitoring service with BT, Britain's largest Internet broadband provider.

NebuAd and Front Porch declined to name the U.S. service providers they are working with, saying it's up to the providers to announce how they deal with consumer data.

Some service providers, such as Embarq and Wide Open West, or WOW, have altered their customer-service agreements to permit the monitoring.

Embarq describes the monitoring as a "preference advertising service." Wide Open West tells customers it is working with a third-party advertising network and names NebuAd as its partner.

Officials at WOW and Embarq declined to talk about any monitoring that has been done.

Each company allows users to opt out of the monitoring, though that permission is buried in customer service documents. The opt-out systems work by planting a "cookie," or a small file left on a user's computer. Each uses a cookie created by NebuAd.

Officials at another service provider, Knology, said it was working with NebuAd and is conducting a test of deep-packet inspection on "several hundred" customers in a service area it declined to identify.

"I don't view it as violating any privacy data at all," said Anthony Palermo, vice present of marketing at Knology. "My understanding is that all these companies go through great pains to hash out information that is specific to the consumer."

One central issue, of course, is how well the companies protect consumer data.

NebuAd promises to protect users' privacy in a couple of ways.

First, every user in the NebuAd system is identified by a number that the company assigns rather than an Internet address, which in theory could be traced to a person. The number NebuAd assigns cannot be tracked to a specific address. That way, if the company's data is stolen or leaked, no one could identify customers or the Web sites they've visited, Dykes said.

Nor does NebuAd record a user's visits to pornography or gaming sites or a user's interests in sensitive subjects—such as bankruptcy or a medical condition such as AIDS. The company said it processes but does not look into packets of information that include e-mail or pictures.

What it does do is categorize users into dozens of targeted consumer types, such as a potential car buyer or someone interested in digital cameras.

Dykes noted that by a couple of measures, their system may protect privacy more than such well-known companies as Google. Google stores a user's Internet address along with the searches made from that address. And while Google's mail system processes e-mail and serves ads based on keywords it finds in their text, NebuAd handles e-mail packets but does not look to them for advertising leads.

Such privacy measures aside, however, consumer advocates questioned whether monitored users are properly informed about the practice.

Knology customers, for example, cull the company's 27-page customer service agreement or its terms and condition for service to find a vague reference to its tracking system.

"They're buried in agreements—who reads them?" said David Hallerman, a senior analyst at eMarketer. "The industry is setting itself up by not being totally transparent….The perception is you're being tracked and targeted."

Things to Think About

1. What risks does industry undertake by being vague about their tracking and monitoring systems? Is it ethical for Internet Service Providers to engage in deep-packet inspection without openly notifying customers? If ISPs are not "telling," how are we aware that deep packet inspection exists?

2. How do advocates of deep-packet inspection rationalize this practice as a benefit to consumers?

3. What is the ethical responsibility of the firms profiting from monitoring customer data packets to inform customers? How do you feel about their adage that they do not hold accountability for what they do—that it is only the responsibility of the ISP?

4. Is it surprising that BT will launch a monitoring service for its customers? Why might this be found to be more controversial in Great Britain than in the United States?

5. NebuAd promises not to look into customer data packets that include email or pictures. Do you find that promise reassuring? How does NebuAd claim to organize its data?

Key Terms

1. Deep-packet inspection

2. Cookie

FORUM 25
Computer Databarges

A nchors Aweigh, my boys and girls...we "save" at break of day-ay-ay-ay. Yes, Google saves data in the sea!

Have you ever wondered just where all of that data that is entered every day is saved? Kevin Kelly of *Wired Magazine* points out that today the Web enables 8 terabytes per second of traffic, 100 billion clicks per day, and 55 trillion links. He reports that the machine is very equivalent to the size and scale of the human brain, and like the human brain, uses associative memory and is roughly equivalent to its size and scope, holding almost the same number of neurons. Since the web doubles in size every 2 years (as theorized and indicated by Moore's Law), if we label the information available today as 1 HB (Human Brain), Kelly advocates that 30 years from now, its size will be 6 billion HB (Kelly, 2009). Thus, the need for data storage is mounting and Google has been praised for its creative solution.

This solution provides other incentives for Google and industry leaders like them. It represents a *green* alternative as it includes using wave energy to power and cool its supercomputer systems used to store data. Data centers consume much energy and leave carbon footprints.

The solution also lowers costs and increases profitability in another manner. Google won't be paying property taxes normally charged for data centers held on land. As for hurricane insurance, that may be another matter!

Article: Google Search Finds Seafaring Solution

By Murad Ahmed
Times Online
September 15, 2008

Google may take its battle for global domination to the high seas with the launch of its own "computer navy".

The company is considering deploying the supercomputers necessary to operate its internet search engines on barges anchored up to seven miles (11km) offshore.

The "water-based data centres" would use wave energy to power and cool their computers, reducing Google's costs. Their offshore status would also mean the company would no longer have to pay property taxes on its data centres, which are sited across the world, including in Britain.

In the patent application seen by *The Times*, Google writes: "Computing centres are located on a ship or ships, anchored in a water body from which energy from natural motion of the water may be captured, and turned into electricity and/or pumping power for cooling pumps to carry heat away."

The increasing number of data centres necessary to cope with the massive information flows generated on popular websites has prompted companies to look at radical ideas to reduce their running costs.

The supercomputers housed in the data centres, which can be the size of football pitches, use massive amounts of electricity to ensure they do not overheat. As a result the internet is not very green.

Data centres consumed 1 per cent of the world's electricity in 2005. By 2020 the carbon footprint of the computers that run the internet will be larger than that of air travel, a recent study by McKinsey, a consultancy firm, and the Uptime Institute, a think tank, predicted.

In an attempt to address the problem, Microsoft has investigated building a data centre in the cold climes of Siberia, while in Japan the technology firm Sun Microsystems plans to send its computers down an abandoned coal mine, using water from the ground as a coolant. Sun said it could save $9 million (£5 million) of electricity costs a year and use half the power the data centre would have required if it was at ground level.

Technology experts said Google's "computer navy" was an unexpected but clever solution. Rich Miller, the author of the datacentreknowledge.com blog, said: "It's really innovative, outside-the-box thinking."

Google refused to say how soon its barges could set sail. The company said: "We file patent applications on a variety of ideas. Some of those ideas later mature into real products, services or infrastructure, some don't."

Concerns have been raised about whether the barges could withstand an event such as a hurricane. Mr Miller said: "The huge question raised by this proposal is how to keep the barges safe."

Things to Think About

1. Explain how Google's solution to storing data is a green alternative. Exactly how does the process work?

2. How does the use of supercomputers leave a carbon footprint? Explain.

3. Why does Google no longer need to pay property taxes on the databarges? Explain.

4. What dangers might be present in this alternative?

5. Will this alternative need regulation in the event of growth in this area? Explain.

Key Terms

1. Wave energy

2. Databarge

FORUM 26
Cyber Weapons: Distributed Denial of Service

W ord association research is often used by marketers to ensure that an appropriate message is received by prospective customers. Original product names are often changed due to negative customer perceptions related to a product name. A noted case was when Dr. James G. Sheehan, a business professor at the University of Cincinnati, led the market research for Kenner Toy Company following lagging sales of a product called the Safety Bake Oven. When concerns for safety were revealed by mothers who were the subjects of the research, the word "safety" was replaced with "easy" in 1963. The Easy Bake Oven went on to become one of the best selling toys ever produced. Indeed, the choice of words used to describe an unfamiliar thing or event may hold considerable power over our perception of its threat to our safety. However, when that misunderstanding minimizes a situation that involves great risk or affects necessary action for real threats, there is urgent cause for concern. Most of us realize the dangers created by agreeing to carry a package for a stranger inside a public building, for example. But when threats to our nation's security are delivered in cyber space, does the general population recognize them and act appropriately?

To learn whether the perceptions of my students appeared accurate, I decided to use what is known as the word association game. When I stated a specific word, my students were directed to indicate the first word that came to their minds. I began with a few innocuous practice words. For example, the word "sun" elicited "summer," "hot," and "burn." "Happy" brought responses of "sad," "smiles," and "fun." However, when I said "war," the word for which I was testing, students responded with "combat," "death," "guns," "camouflage," "blood," and "tanks." Not one student in two sections mentioned any words related to technology.

Could it be that the traditional concept of war is so embedded in our culture that even technology students often dismiss the power and destruction of cyber weaponry? When I hear "war," I think of "computers," "viruses," "Trojans," "botnets," and "Web sites," because I realize that when political and military conflicts erupt between nations, it is Web sites that now appear to be the target. Distributed Denial of Service (DDoS) attacks include the hijacking of an entire network of computers and Web sites. They are transformed into botnets, producing huge streams of random data over the Internet, disabling entire corporate networks.

Recently, a click to open an email attachment, or to open a URL to a rogue Web site, was believed to have set off a seriously disruptive malware program, called the ghost RAT program. It included a feature for turning on the Web cameras and microphones on computers in order to secretly record conversations and activities in a room and gain control of mail servers. There were over 1,200 computers in more than 100 countries infected, including Taiwan, Vietnam, Iran, Bangladesh, Latvia, Indonesia, Philippines, South Korea, Germany, Pakistan, and the United States (Markoff, 2009).

The fact that the text of the email was written successfully to lure recipients to open the attachments and link to URLs is of great concern to security experts. This practice is referred to as social phishing. Social phishing, combined with malware, is now referred to as social malware. All it takes is one person in an organization to fall victim and give the attackers their first foothold. The attackers are believed to have used the social information they gained from email "to send plausible phish." They stole mail in transit and replaced their attachments with toxic ones (malware payloads). The payloads were .doc and .pdf files that installed rootkits on the machines of the Tibetan monks who clicked on them (Anderson and Nagaraja, 2009).

The bottom line is that the informal security model used in this organization is the same used in many organizations and it failed. It consisted of *discretionary access control* in which users are trusted to use their computer resources wisely. "The handling of sensitive data was thus inadequately separated from risky activities—activities that require the user to trust content from strangers" (Anderson and Nagaraja, 2009). A well written technical report providing explicit details can be found at http://www.cl.cam.ac.uk/techreports/UCAM-CL-TR-746.pdf.

Is it *data* that will be both the projectiles and the lost blood of future wars?

Article: Internet Attacks Grow More Potent

By John Markoff
November 9, 2008
The New York Times

SAN FRANCISCO—Attackers bent on shutting down large Web sites—even the operators that run the backbone of the Internet—are arming themselves with what are effectively vast digital fire hoses capable of overwhelming the world's largest networks, according to a new report on online security.

In these attacks, computer networks are hijacked to form so-called botnets that spray random packets of data in huge streams over the Internet. The deluge of data is meant to bring down Web sites and entire corporate networks. Known as distributed denial of service, or D.D.O.S., attacks, such cyberweapons are now routinely used during political and military conflicts, as in Estonia in 2007 during a political fight with Russia, and in the Georgian-Russian war last summer. Such attacks are also being used in blackmail schemes and political conflicts, as well as for general malicious mischief.

A survey of 70 of the largest Internet operators in North America, South America, Europe and Asia found that malicious attacks were rising sharply and that the individual attacks were growing more powerful and sophisticated, according to the Worldwide Infrastructure Security Report. This report is produced annually by Arbor Networks, a company in Lexington, Mass., that provides tools for monitoring the performance of networks.

The report, which will be released Tuesday, shows that the largest attacks have grown steadily in size to over 40 gigabits, from less than half a megabit, over the last seven years. The largest network connections generally available today carry 10 gigabits of data, meaning that they can be overwhelmed by the most powerful attackers.

The Arbor Networks researchers said a 40-gigabit attack took place this year when two rival criminal cybergangs began quarreling over control of an online Ponzi scheme. "This was, initially, criminal-on-criminal crime though obviously the greatest damage was inflicted on the infrastructure used by the criminals," the network operator wrote in a note on the attack.

The attack employed a method called reflective amplification, which allowed a relatively small number of attack computers to generate a huge stream of data toward a victim. The technique has been in use since 2006.

"We're definitely seeing more targeted attacks toward e-commerce sites," said Danny McPherson, chief security officer for Arbor Networks. "Most enterprises are connected to the Internet with a one-gigabit connection or less. Even a two-gigabit D.D.O.S. attack will take them offline."

Large network operators that run the backbone of the Internet have tried to avoid the problem by building excess capacity into their networks, said Edward G. Amoroso, the chief security officer of AT&T. He likened the approach to a large shock absorber, but said he still worried about the growing scale of the attacks.

"We have a big shock absorber," he said. "It works, but it's not going to work if there's some Pearl Harbor event."

Over all, the operators reported they were growing more able to respond to D.D.O.S. attacks because of improved collaboration among service providers.

According to the Arbor Networks report, the network operators said the largest botnets—which in some cases encompass millions of "zombie" computers—continue to "outpace containment efforts and infrastructure investment."

Despite a drastic increase in the number of attacks, the percentage referred to law enforcement authorities declined. The report said 58 percent of the Internet service providers had referred no instances to law enforcement in the last 12 months. When asked why there were so few referrals, 29 percent said law enforcement had limited capabilities, 26 percent said they expected their customers to report illegal activities and 17 percent said there was "little or no utility" in reporting attacks.

Things to Think About

1. How is a denial of service attack different from a distributed denial of service attack? Explain.

2. Many studies have demonstrated that although IS personnel realize the violation to privacy in reading email messages of those they serve in organizations, most admit that curiosity sometimes gets the best of them. Is there any way of controlling this?

3. Explain how it is possible for terrorists to communicate outside the country without the need for access to modes of communication used inside the country and open to government access.

4. Kevin Kelly of *Wired* magazine has discussed the future of the Internet in terms of accessibility to almost any information. What changes may need to be made to better secure information that must be kept private?

5. Why do you think it is that even technology students still do not instinctively think of technology when describing war?

Key Terms

1. Social phishing

2. Malware payloads

FORUM 27
Electronic Mail Snooping

"Curiosity killed the cat," my mother would remind you if you were caught seeking information that was considered "none of your business." We did not dream of opening another person's mail. Beyond the clear ethical violation, it was and is a violation of federal law. But for the digital generation, the ethics and consequences may not be as apparent. On the one hand, our students are told that reading another individual's email is a serious crime. On the other hand, our students are warned that marketers are keeping track of every click they make. Does this seem contradictory?

I recently offered my first year Information Technology students a challenge. "Try to imagine that when you return to your dorm today, a few of your suitemates will be sitting at a computer exhibiting animated emotions of surprise and amusement. When they notice you have arrived, they immediately inform you that they have just discovered the password to a United States vice presidential candidate's email account. They ask you if you would like to see the email. What would you do?"

Instantly, 25 solemn faces became vibrant with passion as they vied to compete for the chance to verbally respond. "Yeah"; "Of course"; "Duuuuh…"; "Did somebody find it?"

By the end of our class session, my students appeared to have a remarkable change of heart over how they would react, especially upon learning the consequences experienced by the real perpetrator of the real exploit of the real candidate, Sarah Palin. However, one cannot conclude that knowledge alone will keep everyone from acting illegally to snoop on the electronic mail of another person.

One recent example was particularly disheartening. Having lived in the Philadelphia region for many years, my favorite television news anchors were Alycia Lane and Larry Mendte. Most assuredly, viewers like me were astounded when a talented, knowledgeable, reputable professional, so familiar with current topics and legal issues related to technology, might involve himself in reading a private citizen's electronic mail—an act that may have caused the destruction of two careers and untold agony for family members.

How could this have been avoided? Did the reporter understand that the breadcrumbs of evidence would be present? Could these cases suggest that an effort to educate consumers technically is an exercise in futility in the absence of teaching ethics?

Article: Fired Philly TV anchor admits hacking e-mail

August 22, 2008
Associated Press

PHILADELPHIA—A fired TV newscaster admitted Friday that he hacked into his co-anchor's e-mail accounts, pleading guilty to one count of illegally accessing a computer.

Larry Mendte admitted that he illegally viewed hundreds of Alycia Lane's e-mails from March 2006 to May 2008, at a time when leaked information about her personal life contributed to her downfall.

Mendte and Lane co-anchored evening broadcasts together for four years at KYW-TV, the CBS affiliate in Philadelphia, until Lane's arrest in December after an alleged scuffle with New York police.

Months later, Mendte was fired and charged by federal prosecutors. His attorney, Michael Schwartz, has said Mendte cooperated from the start.

Mendte faces a maximum possible sentence of five years in prison but is likely to get much less under federal guidelines when he is sentenced Nov. 24. Prosecutors have agreed not to recommend any sentence.

Mendte declined to comment after his plea.

Prosecutors say Mendte accessed three of Lane's e-mail accounts from home and work more than 500 times between January and May of this year alone. Lane's attorney believes he acted out of jealousy.

The allegations are the latest embarrassment for the station, which had been making gains with the Mendte-Lane duo against longtime news leader WPVI-TV, the ABC affiliate.

Mendte, 51, was fired in June after FBI agents searched his home and seized his computer.

According to the criminal information filed in July, Mendte relayed details about Lane's criminal case and other information to a Philadelphia Daily News reporter.

Lane was also fired. She is suing the station over her dismissal, which the station said was necessary because she had become the subject of several news stories.

New York prosecutors in February downgraded felony charges that Lane struck the officer. A judge pledged to drop the remaining charges in August if she is not arrested again.

Mendte, who is married to local Fox news anchor Dawn Stensland, joined the station in July 2003 after several years at the local NBC affiliate. He previously co-hosted "Access Hollywood" and worked at stations in Chicago, San Diego and New York.

Things to Think About

1. Does this case represent an ignorance of the technology that supports the audit trail associated with using a computer? In other words, could it be that Larry did not know that his behavior could be easily determined?

2. Larry gained access to three different personal and business accounts. How might Larry have gained access to Alycia's email? What were the possibilities?

3. What are the consequences of Larry's actions under the law?

4. What message can this case bring to others? Do you believe that technical information and legal issues can prevent such acts? Explain.

5. Are there those who will break the law and engage in high risk behavior even when the consequences are well understood? Explain.

Key Terms

1. Electronic snooping

2. Computer ethics

FORUM 28
Moore's Law and Technology Predictions

Moore's Law was an observation made in 1965 by Gordon Moore, co-founder of Intel. He found that the number of transistors per square inch on integrated circuits had doubled every year since the integrated circuit was invented, increasing processing speed and diminishing costs. In recent years, data density has doubled every 18 months, which is the current definition, and it is predicted that it will continue to do so for the next two decades. The data communications industry has recently been on the same curve.

Recently, you may have noticed an onslaught of television advertising by IBM, a company who would like to use technology to predict advancements in services by creating "service systems." IBM plans to use algorithms to produce a computer model created to determine ways to improve services globally. Its goal is to create a system for which Moore's Law would again apply, one in which a client may see "twice as much efficiency, every two years." For example, "a change in the price of toasters in China affects people in other countries who supply the metal used for the toaster's paneling, and others who produce the plastic, and so on." Jim Spohrer of IBM has estimated that the earth holds more than six trillion service systems and hopes to see the design of systems "that are more self-correcting and can learn" (Vance, 2009). Thus, Moore's Law appears to have become more than just an observation; in some arenas, it suggests a benchmark, while in others, it proves successful in providing accurate predictions.

About 10 years ago, the *Wall Street Journal* asked a group of "experts" to make technology predictions for the future. It was their job to determine the state of technology in 10 years—2008. When it came to making determinations that were predicated on Moore's Law, such as advancements in hardware and network speed, they were right on target. Is it any wonder that when it came to social issues, such as the development of YouTube or the slow progression of online education, they most assuredly missed the mark?

Article: Predictions of the Past: How did we do the last time we looked ahead 10 years? Well, you win some, you lose some.

By George Anders
January 28, 2008
The Wall Street Journal

Here's what 2008 was supposed to look like: Millions of people would use cellphones embedded in their watches or necklaces; devices would translate languages so quickly and so flawlessly that nobody would study foreign languages anymore; telemarketing would be history, as marketers developed better forms of customer prospecting.

Never mind.

Back in 1998, The Wall Street Journal asked dozens of technology-industry executives, scholars and forecasters to guess what the world would be like 10 years later. They took leaps into the unknown, producing what turned out to be a fascinating blend of clever calls and maddening misfires.

Now that the results are in, it's clear that the prognosticators were on safest ground when predicting details about the raw capabilities of high-tech devices. But the seers had a harder time predicting how this fast-changing technology would alter people's habits at work and play.

The most elusive insight: the public's desire to move beyond passive consumption of digital technology, in favor of active creation and sharing of personally shaped content. Forecasters didn't foresee anything resembling the rise of YouTube, Wikipedia, MySpace and incessant blogging.

To their credit, some of 1998's forecasters correctly anticipated that social dynamics would be the hardest part of the puzzle to get right. As Ambuj Goyal, then vice president for systems and software at International Business Machines Corp., remarked a decade ago: "We have predicted the hardware speeds and feeds very well. We haven't done nearly as well in predicting how these machines will be used."

Bearing out Mr. Goyal's point, computer mavens astutely predicted that by 2008, the most powerful desktop computers would run at processing speeds of four gigahertz, while operating with eight gigabytes of random-access memory. Both of those capabilities sounded stunning: They were 100 times the norms of 1998.

No problem. On its Web site, Dell Inc. recently offered high-end desktop computers that run at three gigahertz, with four gigabytes of RAM. By the time 2008 is finished, it is a safe bet that the forecasters' full targets will have been met.

Futurists also predicted that wireless phone calls would get a lot cheaper (correct!) while overall mobile-phone penetration in the U.S. would rise to 51%, up from 20%. That second half of the prediction actually proved too timid. Researchers at SNL Kagan recently estimated that 84% of the U.S. population has mobile phones.

Give the 1998 panelists credit, too, for correctly predicting that Internet access would become ubiquitous, with people able to check their stock quotes from Borneo if they wanted.

When predicting what we would actually do with all that connectivity, however, the prognosticators stumbled. They got hung up, for instance, on ideas such as highly customized advertising, which hasn't made much headway in the face of privacy concerns, and online grocery shopping, which carries too many extra costs to pay its way in most cases.

The experts thought something big was coming in music, most likely new services from recording studios that would let consumers download music onto personal players. They were right about downloadable music—but they couldn't foresee that intermediaries such as Apple Inc., with its wildly popular iPods, would become the preferred way that fans bought their music.

Meanwhile, forecasters in 1998 thought that electronic books would win sweeping acceptance. Old-fashioned paper tomes were supposed to vanish in the face of competition from downloadable manuscripts, viewed on hand-held screens.

What the forecasters didn't appreciate was how hard it would be for electronic books to match the high contrast and easy readability of traditional printed alternatives. Lots of screen-based book readers have been tried—with Amazon.com Inc. introducing the latest version a few months ago. But public acceptance so far has been minimal.

In education, expectations were that distance learning would gain favor, that conventional campuses might atrophy, and that millions of students world-wide might flock to hear star professors' lectures online. Forecasters didn't distinguish between learning at prestigious universities and the nuts-and-bolts tasks of vocational training at companies; they thought trends would play out quickly in both settings.

In fact, online technology's impact on college life hasn't been nearly as revolutionary as expected. While lots of library resources are online and email is ubiquitous, full-time students still want the prestige—and the social benefits—of mingling in person with their peers and professors.

Instead, online education has had its biggest impact in the workplace. There, bosses and employees want to cover necessary ground with a minimum of fuss. In such situations, the faster and cheaper aspects of online tutorials have been irresistible.

The 1998 forecasters also flubbed their attempts to guess which countries would benefit most from the emerging digital economy. They nodded briefly at the idea that better online capability would encourage the outsourcing of tasks to cheaper-wage locations, but didn't foresee the rise of a high-tech service sector in India. Nor did the experts anticipate how rapid, cheap communications across the Pacific would help China align its fast-growing factories with the appetites of U.S. consumers.

Instead one guru argued that the Dutch would fare best. His rationale—which didn't quite pan out—was that their mercantile heritage would be well-suited to the information age.

Asked to pick areas that wouldn't change as fast as many people expected, some experts placed their bets on banking practices. They contended that personal checks would remain the dominant household payment mechanism, in spite of widespread fanfare about new payment systems.

Oops! A Federal Reserve study released in December 2007 found that more than two-thirds of all noncash payments were made electronically. Use of debit cards, online banking and credit cards vastly exceeded the volume of checks written. Even when people paid with old-fashioned checks, paper usually gave way to digital images partway through the settlement process, according to Clearing House Payments Co.

At times, the forecasters were simply too serious for their own good. One predicted that people would use the Internet to monitor their light bulbs and order replacements right away if a bulb burned out. We could do that, but why bother? It's nowhere near as much fun as circulating YouTube videos of crazy wedding dancers.

As Silicon Valley inventor and technologist Judy Estrin gamely conceded in 1998: "What technology can deliver and what people want are two different things."

Things to Think About

1. Specifically which predictions were inaccurate? Would you have made the same mistake? Would students of the digital generation have been able to make these predictions accurately?

2. What are your hardware and software predictions for the future? Create a list of predictions for hardware technology using Moore's Law as a basis for your predictions to 10 years from today.

3. What are your predictions for social and educational uses of technology? Create a list of these predictions to 10 years from now.

4. Could the *Wall Street Journal*'s predictions have been more successful with additional experts from different disciplines? Explain.

5. Kevin Kelly of *Wired Magazine* suggests that since the Web doubles in size every 2 years (as theorized and indicated by Moore's Law), if we label the information available today as 1 HB (Human Brain), then 30 years from now, its size will be 6 billion HB. Kelly suggests, "We did not expect the Impossible." On a presentation slide he purports, "The first lesson of the Web: We have to get better in believing the IMPOSSIBLE" (Kelly, 2008). Do you agree?

Key Words

1. Moore's Law

2. HB

FORUM 29
Computer Waste

Many consumers and institutions upgrade their electronics, including cell phones and computers, on a basis that is in keeping with Moore's Law—about every 18 to 24 months. Most consumers fail to recognize the importance of properly disposing their old, unused, equipment.

Ewaste is highly toxic. It is often outsourced to firms who claim to dispose of it properly. Instead, it is often shipped to third world countries where destitute workers risk their lives to dispose of it.

Is this technology's *dirty* little secret?

Article: Following The Trail Of Toxic E-Waste: 60 Minutes Follows America's Toxic Electronic Waste As It Is Illegally Shipped To Become China's Dirty Secret

November 9, 2008
CBS News

60 Minutes is going to take you to one of the most toxic places on Earth—a place government officials and gangsters don't want you to see. It's a town in China where you can't breathe the air or drink the water, a town where the blood of the children is laced with lead.

It's worth risking a visit because much of the poison is coming out of the homes, schools and offices of America. This is a story about recycling - about how your best intentions to be green can be channeled into an underground sewer that flows from the United States and into the wasteland.

That wasteland is piled with the burning remains of some of the most expensive, sophisticated stuff that consumers crave. And *60 Minutes* and **correspondent Scott Pelley** discovered that the gangs who run this place wanted to keep it a secret.

What are they hiding? The answer lies in the first law of the digital age: newer is better. In with the next thing, and out with the old TV, phone or computer. All of this becomes obsolete, electronic garbage called "e-waste."

Computers may seem like sleek, high-tech marvels. But what's inside them?

"Lead, cadmium, mercury, chromium, polyvinyl chlorides. All of these materials have known toxicological effects that range from brain damage to kidney disease to mutations, cancers," Allen Hershkowitz, a senior scientist and authority on waste management at the Natural Resources Defense Council, explained.

"The problem with e-waste is that it is the fastest-growing component of the municipal waste stream worldwide," he said.

Asked what he meant by "fastest-growing," Hershkowitz said. "Well, we throw out about 130,000 computers every day in the United States."

And he said over 100 million cell phones are thrown out annually.

At a recycling event in Denver, *60 Minutes* found cars bumper-to-bumper for blocks, in a line that lasted for hours. They were there to drop off their computers, PDAs, TVs and other electronic waste.

Asked what he thought happens once his e-waste goes into recycling, one man told Pelley, "Well my assumption is they break it apart and take all the heavy metals and out and then try to recycle some of the stuff that's bad."

Most folks in line were hoping to do the right thing, expecting that their waste would be recycled in state-of-the-art facilities that exist here in America. But really, there's no way for them to know where all of this is going. The recycling industry is exploding and, as it turns out, some so-called recyclers are shipping the waste overseas, where it's broken down for the precious metals inside.

Executive Recycling, of Englewood, Colo., which ran the Denver event, promised the public on its Web site: "Your e-waste is recycled properly, right here in the U.S.—not simply dumped on somebody else."

That policy helped Brandon Richter, the CEO of Executive Recycling, win a contract with the city of Denver and expand operations into three western states.

Asked what the problem is with shipping this waste overseas, Richter told **Pelley**, "Well, you know, they've got low-income labor over there. So obviously they don't have all of the right materials, the safety equipment to handle some of this material."

Executive does recycling in-house, but *60 Minutes* was curious about shipping containers that were leaving its Colorado yard. *60 Minutes* found one container filled with monitors. They're especially hazardous because each picture tube, called a cathode ray tube or CRT, contains several pounds of lead. It's against U.S. law to ship them overseas without special permission. *60 Minutes* took down the container's number and followed it to Tacoma, Wash., where it was loaded on a ship.

When the container left Tacoma, *60 Minutes* followed it for 7,459 miles to Victoria Harbor, Hong Kong.

It turns out the container that started in Denver was just one of thousands of containers on an underground, often illegal smuggling route, taking America's electronic trash to the Far East.

Our guide to that route was Jim Puckett, founder of the Basel Action Network, a watchdog group named for the treaty that is supposed to stop rich countries from dumping toxic waste on poor ones. Puckett runs a program to certify ethical recyclers. And he showed *60 Minutes* what's piling up in Hong Kong.

"It's literally acres of computer monitors," Pelley commented. "Is it legal to import all of these computer monitors into Hong Kong?"

"No way. It is absolutely illegal, both from the standpoint of Hong Kong law but also U.S. law and Chinese law. But it's happening," Puckett said.

60 Minutes followed the trail to a place Puckett discovered in southern China—a sort of Chernobyl of electronic waste—the town of Guiyu. But we weren't there very long before we were picked up by the cops and taken to City Hall. We told the mayor we wanted to see recycling.

So he personally drove us to a shop.

"Let me explain what's happening here," Pelley remarked while in Guiyu. "We were brought into the mayor's office. The mayor told us that we're essentially not welcome here, but he would show us one place where computers are being dismantled and this is that place. A pretty tidy shop. The mayor told us that we would be welcome to see the rest of the town, but that the town wouldn't be prepared for our visit for another year.

"So we were allowed to shoot at that location for about five minutes," Pelley explained further. "And we're back in the mayor's car headed back to City Hall, where I suspect we'll be given another cup of tea and sent on our way out of town with a police escort no doubt."

And we were. But the next day, in a different car and on a different road, we got in.

"This is really the dirty little secret of the electronic age," Jim Puckett said.

Greenpeace has been filming around Guiyu and caught the recycling work. Women were heating circuit boards over a coal fire, pulling out chips and pouring off the lead solder. Men were using what is literally a medieval acid recipe to extract gold. Pollution has ruined the town. Drinking water is trucked in. Scientists have studied the area and discovered that Guiyu has the highest levels of cancer-causing dioxins in the world. They found pregnancies are six times more likely to end in miscarriage, and that seven out of ten kids have too much lead in their blood.

"These people are not just working with these materials, they're living with them. They're all around their homes," Pelley told Allen Hershkowitz.

"The situation in Guiyu is actually pre-capitalist. It's mercantile. It reverts back to a time when people lived where they worked, lived at their shop. Open, uncontrolled burning of plastics. Chlorinated and brominated plastics is known worldwide to cause the emission of polychlorinated and polybrominated dioxins. These are among the most toxic compounds known on earth," Hershkowitz explained.

"We have a situation where we have 21st century toxics being managed in a 17th century environment."

The recyclers are peasant farmers who couldn't make a living on the land. Destitute, they've come by the thousands to get $8 a day. Greenpeace introduced us to some of them. They were afraid and didn't want to be seen, but theirs are the hands that are breaking down America's computers.

"The air I breathe in every day is so pungent I can definitely feel it in my windpipe and affecting my lungs. It makes me cough all the time," one worker told Pelley, with the help of a translator.

"If you're worried about your lungs and you're burning your hands, do you ever think about giving this up?" Pelley asked.

"Yes, I have thought of it," the worker said.

Asked why he doesn't give it up, the worker told him, "Because the money's good."

"You know, it struck me, talking to those workers the other day, that they were destitute and they're happy to have this work," Pelley told Puckett.

"Well, desperate people will do desperate things," Puckett replied. "But we should never put them in that situation. You know, it's a hell of a choice between poverty and poison. We should never make people make that choice."

Pelley, Puckett, and the *60 Minutes* team passed by a riverbed that had been blackened by the ash of burned e-waste.

"Oh, man, this is—it's unbelievably acrid and choking," Pelley said, coughing.

"This is an ash river. This is detritus from burning all this material and this is what the kids get to play in," Puckett explained.

After a few minutes in the real recycling area, we were jumped.

Several men struggled for our cameras. The mayor hadn't wanted us to see this place, and neither did the businessmen who were profiting from it. They got a soil sample that we'd taken for testing, but we managed to wrestle the cameras back.

What were they afraid of?

"They're afraid of being found out," Puckett said. "This is smuggling. This is illegal. A lot of people are turning a blind eye here. And if somebody makes enough noise, they're afraid this is all gonna dry up."

Back in Denver, there's no threat of it drying up. In fact, it was a flood.

And Brandon Richter, CEO of Executive Recycling, was still warning of the dangers of shipping waste to China. "I just heard actually a child actually died over there breaking this material down, just getting all these toxins," he said.

Then Pelley told him we'd tracked his container to Hong Kong.

"This is a photograph from your yard, the Executive Recycling yard," Pelley told Richter, showing him a photo we'd taken of a shipping container in his yard. "We followed this container to Hong Kong."

"Okay," Richter replied.

"And I wonder why that would be?" Pelley asked.

"Hmm. I have no clue," Richter said.

"The Hong Kong customs people opened the container…and found it full of CRT screens which, as you probably know, is illegal to export to Hong Kong," Pelley said.

"Yeah, yep," Richter replied. "I don't know if that container was filled with glass. I doubt it was. We don't fill glass, CRT glass in those containers."

"This container was in your yard, filled with CRT screens, and exported to Hong Kong, which probably wouldn't be legal," Pelley said.

"No, absolutely not. Yeah," Richter said.

"Can you explain that?" Pelley asked.

"Yeah, it's not—it was not filled in our facility," Richter said.

But that's where *60 Minutes* filmed it. And we weren't the only ones asking questions. It turns out Hong Kong customs intercepted the container and sent it back to Executive Recycling, Englewood, Colorado, the contents listed as "waste: cathode ray tubes."

U.S. customs x-rayed the container and found the same thing. *60 Minutes* showed Richter this evidence, and later his lawyer told us the CRTs were exported under Executive Recycling's name, but without the company's permission.

"I know this is your job," Richter told Pelley. "But, unfortunately, you know, when you attack small business owners like this and you don't have all your facts straight, it's unfortunate, you know?"

But here's one more fact: the federal Government Accountability Office set up a sting in which U.S. investigators posed as foreign importers. Executive Recycling offered to sell 1,500 CRT computer monitors and 1,200 CRT televisions to the GAO's fictitious broker in Hong Kong. But Executive Recycling was not alone. The GAO report found that another 42 American companies were willing to do the same.

Things to Think About

1. Explain how electronic waste is toxic?

2. What are the costs associated with the elimination of ewaste? Is it necessary for organizations to work this cost into their budgets?

3. How does your organization dispose of electronic waste and at what cost?

4. What are the legal issues involved in the elimination of ewaste?

5. What are the ethical and health issues for those working and living near locations where waste is stored?

Key Terms

1. Ewaste

2. Electronic toxins

FORUM 30
Reality Mining

How entropic (predictable) are most people's lives? (http://reality.media.mit.edu). Only your Bluetooth knows for sure! Reality mining is the study of human interaction based on the use of portable computing devices to passively record and measure data, providing insight into individual and group behavior. It is a form of data mining that extracts hidden patterns from "real" data. "The purpose is to get a more accurate picture of what people do, where people go, and with whom they communicate from a device they carry than from more subjective sources, including what people say about themselves. In short, people lie—cell phones, don't" (Hesseldahl, 2008).

Using Bluetooth, the short-range technology that creates wireless connections between electronic sensors, reality mining has proven beneficial in providing a wide range of solutions. It has been used to predict the effects of a terrorist attack on the Golden Gate Bridge, by monitoring traffic patterns. It is used to monitor and track health concerns, such as flu trends, by monitoring search queries for flu-related symptoms. Traffic patterns are determined with much greater accuracy by using GPS chips to track location. Built-in microphones can be used to diagnose depression, found by analysis of the way a person talks. An accelerometer in the phone that measures whether a person is sitting or walking, can detect the gait of a person, to indicate the possibility of Parkinson's disease. The benefits seem endless.

But so does its propensity for abuse! Reality mining also can be used to collect intelligence information that can be misused by a variety of organizations, including insurance companies who may deny coverage and government agencies, to track social networks.

Dr. Mallone, of the MIT Media Lab reminds us, "For most of human history, people lived in small tribes where everything they did was known by everyone they knew…Privacy may turn out to have become an anomaly" (Markoff, 2008).

Are you ready to be a member of a global tribe?

Article: You're Leaving a Digital Trail. What About Privacy?

By John Markoff
The New York Times
November 30, 2008

HARRISON BROWN, an 18-year-old freshman majoring in mathematics at M.I.T., didn't need to do complex calculations to figure out he liked this deal: in exchange for letting researchers track his every move, he receives a free smartphone.

Now, when he dials another student, researchers know. When he sends an e-mail or text message, they also know. When he listens to music, they know the song. Every moment he has his Windows Mobile smartphone with him, they know where he is, and who's nearby.

Mr. Brown and about 100 other students living in Random Hall at M.I.T. have agreed to swap their privacy for smartphones that generate digital trails to be beamed to a central computer. Beyond individual actions, the devices capture a moving picture of the dorm's social network.

The students' data is but a bubble in a vast sea of digital information being recorded by an ever thicker web of sensors, from phones to GPS units to the tags in office ID badges, that capture our movements and interactions. Coupled with information already gathered from sources like Web surfing and credit cards, the data is the basis for an emerging field called collective intelligence.

Propelled by new technologies and the Internet's steady incursion into every nook and cranny of life, collective intelligence offers powerful capabilities, from improving the efficiency of advertising to giving community groups new ways to organize.

But even its practitioners acknowledge that, if misused, collective intelligence tools could create an Orwellian future on a level Big Brother could only dream of.

Collective intelligence could make it possible for insurance companies, for example, to use behavioral data to covertly identify people suffering from a particular disease and deny them insurance coverage. Similarly, the government or law enforcement agencies could identify members of a protest group by tracking social networks revealed by the new technology. "There are so many uses for this technology—from marketing to war fighting—that I can't imagine it not pervading our lives in just the next few years," says Steve Steinberg, a computer scientist who works for an investment firm in New York.

In a widely read Web posting, he argued that there were significant chances that it would be misused, "This is one of the most significant technology trends I have seen in years; it may also be one of the most pernicious."

For the last 50 years, Americans have worried about the privacy of the individual in the computer age. But new technologies have become so powerful that protecting individual privacy may no longer be the only issue. Now, with the Internet, wireless sensors, and the capability to analyze an avalanche of data, a person's profile can be drawn without monitoring him or her directly.

"Some have argued that with new technology there is a diminished expectation of privacy," said Marc Rotenberg, executive director of the Electronic Privacy Information Center, a privacy rights group in Washington. "But the opposite may also be true. New techniques may require us to expand our understanding of privacy and to address the impact that data collection has on groups of individuals and not simply a single person."

Mr. Brown, for one, isn't concerned about losing his privacy. The M.I.T researchers have convinced him that they have gone to great lengths to protect any information generated by the experiment that would reveal his identity.

Besides, he says, "the way I see it, we all have Facebook pages, we all have e-mail and Web sites and blogs."

"This is a drop in the bucket in terms of privacy," he adds.

GOOGLE and its vast farm of more than a million search engine servers spread around the globe remain the best example of the power and wealth-building potential of collective intelligence. Google's fabled PageRank algorithm, which was originally responsible for the quality of Google's search results, drew its precision from the inherent wisdom in the billions of individual Web links that people create.

The company introduced a speech-recognition service in early November, initially for the Apple iPhone, that gains its accuracy in large part from a statistical model built from several trillion search terms that its users have entered in the last decade. In the future, Google will take advantage of spoken queries to predict even more accurately the questions its users will ask.

And, a few weeks ago, Google deployed an early-warning service for spotting flu trends, based on search queries for flu-related symptoms.

The success of Google, along with the rapid spread of the wireless Internet and sensors—like location trackers in cellphones and GPS units in cars—has touched off a race to cash in on collective intelligence technologies.

In 2006, Sense Networks, based in New York, proved that there was a wealth of useful information hidden in a digital archive of GPS data generated by tens of thousands of taxi rides in San Francisco. It could see, for example, that people who worked in the city's financial district would tend to go to work early when the market was booming, but later when it was down.

It also noticed that middle-income people—as determined by ZIP code data—tended to order cabs more often just before market downturns.

Sense has developed two applications, one for consumers to use on smartphones like the BlackBerry and the iPhone, and the other for companies interested in forecasting social trends and financial behavior. The consumer application, Citysense, identifies entertainment hot spots in a city. It connects information from Yelp and Google about nightclubs and music clubs with data generated by tracking locations of anonymous cellphone users.

The second application, Macrosense, is intended to give businesses insight into human activities. It uses a vast database that merges GPS, Wi-Fi positioning, cell-tower triangulation, radio frequency identification chips and other sensors.

"There is a whole new set of metrics that no one has ever measured," said Greg Skibiski, chief executive of Sense. "We were able to look at people moving around stores" and other locations. Such travel patterns, coupled with data on incomes, can give retailers early insights into sales levels and who is shopping at competitors' stores.

Alex Pentland, a professor at the Media Lab at the Massachusetts Institute of Technology who is leading the dormitory research project, was a co-founder of Sense Networks. He is part of a new generation of researchers who have relatively effortless access to data that in the past was either painstakingly assembled by hand or acquired from questionnaires or interviews that relied on the memories and honesty of the subjects.

The Media Lab researchers have worked with Hitachi Data Systems, the Japanese technology company, to use some of the lab's technologies to improve businesses' efficiency. For example, by equipping employees with sensor badges that generate the same kinds of data provided by the students' smartphones, the researchers determined that face-to-face communication was far more important to an organization's work than was generally believed.

Productivity improved 30 percent with an incremental increase in face-to-face communication, Dr. Pentland said. The results were so promising that Hitachi has established a consulting business that overhauls organizations via the researchers' techniques.

Dr. Pentland calls his research "reality mining" to differentiate it from an earlier generation of data mining conducted through more traditional methods.

Dr. Pentland "is the emperor of networked sensor research," said Michael Macy, a sociologist at Cornell who studies communications networks and their role as social networks. People and organizations, he said, are increasingly choosing to interact with one another through digital means that record traces of those interactions. "This allows scientists to study those interactions in ways that five years ago we never would have thought we could do," he said.

ONCE based on networked personal computers, collective intelligence systems are increasingly being created to leverage wireless networks of digital sensors and smartphones. In one application, groups of scientists and political and environmental activists are developing "participatory sensing" networks.

At the Center for Embedded Networked Sensing at the University of California, Los Angeles, for example, researchers are developing a Web service they call a Personal Environmental Impact Report to build a community map of air quality in Los Angeles. It is intended to let people assess how their activities affect the environment and to make decisions about their health. Users may decide to change their jogging route, or run at a different time of day, depending on air quality at the time.

"Our mantra is to make it possible to observe what was previously unobservable," said Deborah Estrin, director of the center and a computer scientist at U.C.L.A.

But Dr. Estrin said the project still faced a host of challenges, both with the accuracy of tiny sensors and with the researchers' ability to be certain that personal information remains private. She is skeptical about technical efforts to obscure the identity of individual contributors to databases of information collected by network sensors.

Attempts to blur the identity of individuals have only a limited capability, she said. The researchers encrypt the data to protect against identifying particular people, but that has limits.

"Even though we are protecting the information, it is still subject to subpoena and subject to bullying bosses or spouses," she said.

She says that there may still be ways to protect privacy. "I can imagine a system where the data will disappear," she said.

Already, activist groups have seized on the technology to improve the effectiveness of their organizing. A service called MobileActive helps nonprofit organizations around the world use mobile phones to harness the expertise and the energy of their participants, by sending out action alerts, for instance.

Pachube (pronounced "PATCH-bay") is a Web service that lets people share real-time sensor data from anywhere in the world. With Pachube, one can combine and display sensor data, from the cost of energy in one location, to temperature and pollution monitoring, to data flowing from a buoy off the coast of Charleston, S.C., all creating an information-laden snapshot of the world.

Such a complete and constantly updated picture will undoubtedly redefine traditional notions of privacy.

DR. PENTLAND says there are ways to avoid surveillance-society pitfalls that lurk in the technology. For the commercial use of such information, he has proposed a set of principles derived from English common law to guarantee that people have ownership rights to data about their behavior. The idea revolves around three principles: that you have a right to possess your own data, that you control the data that is collected about you, and that you can destroy, remove or redeploy your data as you wish.

At the same time, he argued that individual privacy rights must also be weighed against the public good.

Citing the epidemic involving severe acute respiratory syndrome, or SARS, in recent years, he said technology would have helped health officials watch the movement of infected people as it happened, providing an opportunity to limit the spread of the disease.

"If I could have looked at the cellphone records, it could have been stopped that morning rather than a couple of weeks later," he said. "I'm sorry, that trumps minute concerns about privacy."

Indeed, some collective-intelligence researchers argue that strong concerns about privacy rights are a relatively recent phenomenon in human history.

"The new information tools symbolized by the Internet are radically changing the possibility of how we can organize large-scale human efforts," said Thomas W. Malone, director of the M.I.T. Center for Collective Intelligence.

"For most of human history, people have lived in small tribes where everything they did was known by everyone they knew," Dr. Malone said. "In some sense we're becoming a global village. Privacy may turn out to have become an anomaly."

Things to Think About

1. List ways in which reality mining can benefit society.

2. How do researchers attempt to protect the identity of their subjects?

3. How does Pachube provide a service to consumers? Explain.

4. What advice does Dr. Pentland give in order to avoid surveillance society pitfalls? Is it pragmatic?

5. Researchers argue that privacy rights are only a relatively recent phenomenon in human history. In terms of ethics, does that matter?

Key Terms

1. Collective intelligence

2. Reality mining

References

Anderson, Ross, and Nagaraja, Shishir. (2009, March). The Snooping Dragon: Social-Malware Surveillance of the Tibetan Movement. UCAM-CL-TR-746, ISSN 1476-2986. *University of Cambridge.*

Arrington, M. (2009, January 5). Celebrity Twitter Accounts Hacked. *Techcrunch.com.*

Austin, R. (2007, September 28). Digital Forensics on the Cheap. ACM Digital Library, Proceedings of the 4th Annual Conference on Information Security Curriculum Development.

Bartlett, John. (1919). Familiar Quotations, 10th Edition.

Blake, E. (2007, September 28). Network Security: VoIP Security on Data Network. ACM Digital Library, Proceedings of the 4th Annual Conference on Information Security Curriculum Development.

Brunker, Mike. (2009, January 15). Sexting Surprise: Teens Face Child Porn Charges. *MSNBC.com.*

Celizik, Mike. (2009, March 6). Her Teen Committed Suicide Over Texting. *MSNBC.com.*

Clifford, S. (2009, January 26). Teaching Teenagers About Harassment. *The New York Times.*

Computer Science and Telecommunications Board. (1999). Being Fluent With Information Technology. Committee on Information Technology Literacy. Commission on Physical Sciences, Mathematics and Applications. National Research Council. *National Academy Press, Washington, D.C.*

Condon, S. (2008, October 10). President Signs Broadband Data Collection Bill. *Cnet News.*

Crovitz, L.G. (2009, April 9). Wikipedia's Old Fashioned Revolution. *The Wall Street Journal.*

Devaney, Laura. (2009, April 10). Why Open Source Library Software is a Trend. *eSchool News.*

FDIC.gov. (2005, Summer). A Changing Rate Environment. *Supervisory Insights.*

Fetterman, M. (2006, August 4). Costly College Prerequisite. *USA Today.*

Firth, N. (2007, October 26). Human Race Will Split. *Sciencetech*.

Foley, M. (2008, December 11). Proposed Web Filter Criticized in Australia. *The New York Times*.

Fox News. (2009, February 25). NYC Official: Ban Japanese Rape Video Game. *FoxNews.com*.

Goldman, E. (2003, August 3). Congress, The New Copyright Bully. *Cnet News*.

Harvey, M. (2009, February 13). Internet Trial of the Decade to Begin. *The New York Times*.

Hart, K. And Whoriskey, P. (2009, February 14). Stalled Switch to Digital TV a Classic Tale of Breakdown. *The Washington Post*.

Hendrickson, M. (2008, May 19). ClearContext's Stab at Making Email More Manageable. *TechCrunch*.

Hesseldahl, Arik. (2008, March 24). There's Gold in Reality Mining. *BusinessWeek*.

Heussner, Ki Mae. (2008, August 14). Leading Computer Scientists Defend Student Hackers. *ABC News*.

Kelly, K. (2009, February 13). Web and Where 2.0 +. *Northern California Grantmakers Conference*.

Kennedy, J. (2009, January). *Digital Music Report*.

Krazil, T. (2008, April 3). Gore: Wireless Access to Info Means Power. *Cnet News*.

Koizumi, K. (2008, March). Historical Trends in Federal R & D. *AAAS Report*.

Komando. (2008). Criminals Have Now Gone Vishing. *USA Today*.

Lakin, M. (2008, October 8). UT Student David Kernell Pleads Not Guilty in Palin E-Mail Hacking. *Knox News*.

Lessig, Lawrence. (2006). Code and Other Laws of CyberSpace. *Basic Books*.

Leyden, John. (2007, November 5). Hack Database, Change School Grades, Go to Jail For 20 Years (Maybe). *The Register*.

Markoff, John. (2009, March 28). Vast Spy System Loots Computers in 103 Countries. *The New York Times*.

Markoff, John. (2008, November 30). You're Leaving a Digital Trail. What About Privacy? *The New York Times*.

Martindale, Scott. (2008, September 16). Tesoro High Computer Hacking Case Moves Toward Trial. *OC Register*.

McAfee, Andrew. (2008, January 14). Why Not Widen The Flow. *Harvard Business School Faculty Blogs*.

McMillan, Robert. (2009, February 2). Industry giants to weigh in on US privacy laws. *Macworld.com*.

Meller, P. (2009, February 13). Social Networking Sites Sign EU Pact on Child Safety. *Techworld.com*.

NBC News. (2007, February 9). High School Hackers Cancel School With Fake Snow Day. *WLWT/NBC News*.

O'Brien, T. (2009, February 12). Ten Ways to Speed Up Your Computer Now. *Switched*.

Oliphant, J. (2009, March 3). Get Out of the Way. *Los Angeles Times*.

Pastor Bob's Blog, (2008). http://blogs.myspace.com/index.cfm?fuseaction=blog.view&friendId=45665414&blogId=463302596.

Prieto, Bianca. (2009, March 11). Teens Learning There Are Consequences to Sexting. *Seattle Times*.

Ramana. (2008, October 2). Bill Gates: Family and Early Childhood, http://www.getyourcontent.com/1/18236-0/BILL-GATES-FAMILY-AND-EAR.aspx.

Riddle, W. (2009, March 10). Australian Private Investigators Offer Illegal Spouse Tracking Services. *Switched*.

Raskin, J. (2003). Overruling Democracy: The Supreme Court vs. The American People. *Routledge*.

Schiffman, B. (2008, April 30). Torture by Information Overload. *Wired Magazine*.

Siwek, S. (2007, August). The True Cost of Sound Recording Piracy to the US Economy. *IPI Publications.nsf*.

South Florida Sun Sentinel. (2008, March 14). Student Accused of Hacking School District Database.

Stanford University. 2005 Commencement.
        (*http://www.youtube.com/watch?v=UF8uR6Z6KLc*).

Telegraph.co.uk. (2009, January 30). Computer Hackers Put Pornography on Primary
        School Websites.

University of Oxford. (2008, March 17). Digital Piracy May Benefit Companies.

Vance, Ashlee. (2009, March 26). A Moore's Law for Technology Services? *The New
        York Times*.

Wagley, John. (2008, September). Private Records. *Security Management*.

Warburton, N. (2008, September 23). Cutting the Cord. *Deseret News*.

Wax, Emily. (2008, December 3). Gunmen Used Technology as a Tactical Tool. *The
        Washington Post*.

Yarden, Jonathan. (2004, August 24). Protect Against Root Exploits in Unix Systems.
        Tech Republic.Oxford, Media
        (http://www.ox.ac.uk/media/news_stories/2008/080317.html).

Credits

This page constitutes an extension of the copyright page. We have made every effort to trace the ownership of all copyrighted material and to secure permission from copyright holders. In the event of any question arising as to the use of any material, we will be pleased to make the necessary corrections in future printings. Thanks are due to the following authors, publishers, and agents for permission to use the material indicated.